ACKN  S

Pastor Tom Hughes has written a must-read book about the decline of our nation from one based on Judeo-Christian values to one captivated by materialism and secularism. It is a fascinating book from start to finish, but it is a sobering one that will drive you into the scriptures and force you to your knees in prayer.

Dr. David R. Reagan
Founder and Senior Evangelist for Lamb and Lion Ministries
Christianprophecy.org

Pastor Tom Hughes has been a personal encouragement to me as a ministry leader. I operate in a world of millions of pastors who do not preach the whole counsel of God. They do not consider Bible prophecy to be relevant today. Thank God for Pastor Tom who covers the topic with unusual expertise.

I get emails from broken-hearted people who are searching and searching for a church and pastor who will talk about these important issues. We're in the "times of the signs". Let's get excited about that as Pastor Tom Hughes does every day. From his EndTimesTV to his books to his pulpit messages, he is truly equipping the saints.

Jan Markell
Founder, President and Host of Understanding the Times
Olivetreeviews.org

"Tom Hughes issues America's report card from a Pastor's perspective. He identifies America's spiritual and moral ailments and then provides the proven biblical prescriptions that can remedy the problems. Pastor Tom responsibly weaves the reader through the fabrics of American society and deposits relevant quotes from great American presidents and patriots along the way. At the end of the story is a potential silver lining of hope, but Pastor Tom clearly points out that America's destiny remains in the hands of its people. America's Coming Judgment officially serves Americans notice that it's time to be accountable to GOD if they want America to be GREAT AGAIN!"

Bill Salus
Founder of Prophecy Depot Ministries
Prophecydepotministries.net

AMERICA'S
COMING JUDGMENT
WHERE IS OUR HOPE?

THOMAS J. HUGHES
TOM GILBREATH

Foreword by Hal Lindsey

America's Coming Judgment
by Thomas J. Hughes
with Tom Gilbreath
All rights reserved.

ISBN: 978-0-9976052-2-8

Printed in the United States of America

TABLE OF CONTENTS

FOREWORD

By Hal Lindsey

FOR AMERICA, THE STAKES KEEP GOING UP. The world's trouble spots become more numerous and perilous every year. Old enemies grow more powerful and more menacing, while new enemies seem to spring up out of nowhere.

A few days before his 30th birthday, Abraham Lincoln told the Young Men's Lyceum of Springfield, Illinois that, in America, "If destruction be our lot, we must ourselves be its author and finisher."

When Walt Disney put those words in his "Great Moments with Mr. Lincoln" show at the 1964 World's Fair, and then at Disneyland, the Cold War was at its height. He knew that Soviet ICBMs with their MIRV warheads could rain down fire on America at a moment's notice.

But Disney also knew what most Americans have always known intuitively — that the security of the United States has more to do with ourselves and our character, than with the supposed strength of our enemies.

The history books claim that the United States and Soviet Union kept nuclear obliteration at bay because of what they called, "the doctrine of Mutual Assured Destruction," or "MAD." But I believe that "doctrine" was inadequate to the task. Our protection during those years was divine. In the early stages of the Cold War, we adopted the motto, "In God We Trust."

The United States was never a "Christian nation" per se. But, for a very long time, it was a nation that rested its hand on the Bible to denote maximum veracity. As this book attests, America's most famous deists, Thomas Jefferson and Benjamin Franklin, carefully studied scripture, and called themselves "Christians."

But the sense of the sacred, in which even American unbelievers once regarded God and the Bible, has passed into history. "It's the Gospel truth," no longer holds special meaning for most Americans. This doesn't just result in empty churches, but in empty souls.

Like so many nations in trouble, America today searches for a savior — usually during presidential elections. But presidents make mistakes. They're only human. And in today's fast-paced world, mistakes grow continually more costly as advances in technology amplify every human frailty.

It's okay to hope that a President will do well, but even the cleverest leader will not be able to heal this nation's ills. Tax policy, healthcare, military spending, and rebuilding America's infrastructure are important. But the real problem is not crumbling bridges or an outdated power grid. The real problem is America's crumbling moral infrastructure.

Is God's judgment coming to America? The nation is already suffering severely because of its rejection of Him and His word. Studies published recently in *JAMA*, the *Journal of the American Medical Association: Psychiatry*, found that alcoholism rose 49% in just eleven years. One in eight Americans received a diagnosis of alcoholism within the last year. How many have yet to be diagnosed?

These extreme levels of alcohol addiction must be looked at in conjunction with a raging opioid epidemic. Add to that, the explosion of marijuana use. Put it all together, and a picture emerges. This nation is trying to self-medicate away its fears, sadness, and anxieties. When people turn from God, they inevitably turn to withering fig leaves in their bid to feel secure, fulfilled, and happy. But only in God do we find lasting solutions to humanity's deepest needs.

What will spiritual renewal look like? It will look like repentance. And, if it happens, I believe it will begin with

Christians and the Church. We, the people of God, need to recognize our rebellion against Him. We need to turn from sin. Political leaders have a part to play, but they are ill-equipped to handle the present crisis because, at heart, it is a moral crisis.

We need men and women of God to boldly proclaim His word. I don't mean that we should be unkind, self-righteous, or smug. We must preach with humility and lovingkindness. Like the faithful of previous generations, we must speak His word, and we must do so in no uncertain terms.

Watching the Orson Welles film version of my book, *The Late Great Planet Earth*, played a key role in the author of this book, Thomas Hughes, coming to Christ. It also sparked his ongoing interest in Bible prophecy. It's a thrilling thing to know that I had a role in all that. I count him as a friend, and fellow-worker in Christ. His co-writer, Tom Gilbreath, has been helping me prepare *The Hal Lindsey Report* for several years.

I believe *America's Coming Judgment* offers crucial insight to anyone who wants to understand our nation's real position in the world — our peril, and our hope.

INTRODUCTION

As I write these words, the American schism of recent years has deepened into something I have never seen before. I suspect we would have to go back to Civil War-era America to find a time when anger and division were this severe.

This century has seen partisanship reach amazing heights — or should I say, depths. It reached those levels even before the election of the most divisive president since Lincoln — Donald John Trump.

The good news for Trump is that many historians consider Lincoln our greatest president. I hope President Trump does as well. But as I write these words, we have more questions than answers.

Like the rest of the country, the followers of Christ have varied opinions regarding the President. Some are euphoric in their belief that God's man has at last arrived in the White House. Others worry that we've elected a fascist. The majority land somewhere in between.

I mention the President here because that's what people bring up to me when we discuss this book. But, to be clear, *America's Coming Judgment* is not an evaluation of Donald Trump as a man or as a President. In fact, it rarely mentions him. Rather, the book evaluates the United States of America according to God's standards as laid out in the Bible. It examines the crucial question — *where are we as a nation before God?*

As you draw your conclusions, I hope you will consider some of the questions this book raises. How grievous are our national sins? Have we, as a people, repented of them? Have we even acknowledged them? Have we gone too far?

I hope you will see in these pages, not only some of the difficulties America faces, but what each of us can and should do about them — for ourselves, and for our young.

Thomas J. Hughes, Hemet, California, 2017

Chapter 1

THE RICH MAN'S TREE

NO WEAPON OF TERROR, no conspiracy of men should ever make the United States of America tremble with fear. But the words of Jesus in Luke 12:48 should.

> For everyone to whom much is given, from him much will be required.

Never has a nation been so blessed — both spiritually and materially — as this one. For most of its history, Americans have rightly believed in their country's unique place in history. They've seen this land as extraordinary. The United States of America was never perfect — not even close. But it was special... *exceptional.*

In his December 1862 address to Congress, Abraham Lincoln called America, "the last best hope of earth."

Ronald Reagan expanded on that thought in the 1964 speech that launched his political career. "You and I have a rendezvous with destiny. We will preserve for our children this, the last best hope of man on earth, or we will sentence them to take the first step into a thousand years of darkness. If we fail, at least let our children and our children's children say of us we justified our brief moment here. We did all that could be done."

Over the last few decades, America has changed in countless ways — some good, many bad. If you've been alive for long, you may at times feel like you've been transported to another planet. In fact, over just the last five years, the culture has changed so much that your head may be spinning. And it's not just the massive level of change. It's the dramatic increase in the rate of change. We see transformative change in all directions — happening fast, and getting faster.

HUMAN WORTH

Before the United States, no nation ever held so firmly to a belief in the rights and dignity of every individual. The country didn't always live up to that ideal. In fact, it failed miserably in lots of areas. It still fails. But with liberty and human worth as a North Star, amazing things were achieved in the last 240-plus years.

Most of the world today agrees with, admires, and aspires to a high level of human rights. That's largely due to the example of the United States. But now, when most of the world embraces these values, they have begun to die. We see human dignity demeaned at every turn. Why? If most of us agree, why are these things disappearing?

Imagine that a rich man finds a big, beautiful tree, and decides to transplant it. The bigger the tree, the more expensive it is to move. This man didn't get rich by wasting money. He decides to transplant only the part of the tree he likes — the trunk, limbs, leaves, and fruit. In other words, he transplants only the visible part of the tree. He cuts it off at ground level. Abandoning the roots, the man moves the lovely tree to his preferred location.

Without roots, of course, the tree dies. Leave only a few roots, and it dies more slowly. Cut the roots slowly but systematically over a period of years, and the tree may appear healthy for a while. But as you sever more connections to the roots, it must eventually die.

BIBLE ROOTS

I will show in the following pages that America's understanding and implementation of the rights and dignity of the individual rises out of a specific root system — respect for the Bible and the teachings of Christ. Cut it off from those roots, and no matter how much you love the tree and want it to thrive, it cannot. An understanding of the unique value of each individual comes from a biblical worldview. Take that away, and human rights begin to wither and die.

Some might point to slavery, or to Jim Crow laws in the United States, to disprove the idea that America ever truly held such values. But human liberty in America was not born full-grown. The ideals espoused in the Declaration of Independence and in the Bill of Rights have yet to be fully realized. So, they were certainly not reached instantly. But those ideals eventually led to slavery's end and, later, to the end of government-sponsored discrimination based on race.

When Dr. Martin Luther King Jr. and others founded an organization to fight for the full rights of citizenship for African-Americans, he named it the "Southern Christian Leadership Conference." Notice the word "Christian" there at its heart.

Dr. King was a Baptist minister. We remember him as one of the greatest speakers in American history. But those of us who have been around church know that this was not ordinary speaking. It was preaching, and it was filled with scriptural touchstones. In organizing mass meetings, he used the model of his friend Billy Graham's crusades.

Like America, Dr. King did not always live up to his ideals. Also like America, at his best, he presented a biblical understanding of human beings and human rights. It may seem obvious, but let me say it anyway. American ideals rose from the Bible — not Freud, Marx, or Nietzsche.

Women's rights, racial equality, and respect for rich and poor alike, flow from the pages of a book written when such things were unprecedented. Jesus taught that all are sinners, and that He would die for the salvation of everyone equally. Galatians 3:28 says that in Christ, "There is neither Jew nor Greek, there is neither slave nor free, there is neither male nor female; for you are all one in Christ Jesus."

Ephesians 2:14 says, "For He Himself is our peace, who has made both one, and has broken down the middle wall of separation."

That is the kind of thinking that informed the ideas that created the nation that is the United States of America. In this book, we will examine America's future. But to do that, we need to visit her past — and her strong connection to a land far away and long ago.

Chapter 2

LAMENT FOR A GREAT NATION

SINCE WELL BEFORE ITS FOUNDING, optimism has been a defining American characteristic. A 2015 article in *The Atlantic* said, "For centuries, visitors to the United States have been struck by the boundless optimism of its people. Recent research bears out the stereotype, confirming that Americans really are more hopeful about the future than their peers in other wealthy nations."[1]

Americans have been drawn to the cheerful, not the sardonic — the happy, not the sad. Europeans have often looked across the Atlantic with dismay that such a wealthy, educated nation could seem like a bunch of happy-go-lucky rubes.

Jules Verne depicted Americans as the ones who would make it to the moon first. In his 1865 novel, *From the Earth to the Moon*, the Frenchman wrote, "Nothing can astound an American.... In America, all is easy, all is simple; and

---

1. "What Makes Americans So Optimistic?" by Jared Keller, *The Atlantic*, March 25, 2015

as for mechanical difficulties, they are overcome before they arise.... No true Yankee would have allowed even the semblance of a difficulty to be possible. A thing with them is no sooner said than done."[2]

AMERICAN CORN

Alexis de Tocqueville, another Frenchman, traveled the United States in the early 19th century. He said Americans "have all a lively faith in the perfectibility of man.... They all consider society as a body in a state of improvement."[3]

In early 2001, Irish philosopher Charles Handy retraced de Tocqueville's journey across America. He wrote, "Anyone visiting America from Europe cannot fail to be struck by the energy, enthusiasm, and confidence in their country's future that he or she will meet among ordinary Americans — a pleasing contrast to the world-weary cynicism of much of Europe. Most Americans seem to believe that the future can be better and that they are responsible for doing their best to make it that way."[4]

Maybe that's why the most successful American entertainment tends to be earnest and hopeful. Look at a list

---

2. *rom the Earth to the Moon* by Jules Verne, 1865

3. *Democracy in America: Part One* by Alexis de Tocqueville, 1835]

4. "Tocqueville Revisited: The Meaning of American Prosperity — Tocqueville's Look at 2001" by Charles Handy. Harvard Business Review, January 2001

of Hollywood's greatest hits. Most have one thing in common — they came straight out of an American field of sweet corn.

We all prefer optimism to pessimism. But in a time like this, we also need realism.

REAGAN AND LINCOLN

One of Hollywood's most inspirational hits was not a film, but a film actor turned politician — President Ronald Reagan. He remains extremely popular with political conservatives and has gained a degree of respect among those of opposite political beliefs, largely based on his optimism.

In his first inaugural address, he asked, "Can we solve the problems confronting us? Well, the answer is an unequivocal and emphatic 'yes.'"

He ran for reelection in 1984. During his acceptance speech at the Republican National Convention that year, he said, "Every promise, every opportunity, is still golden in this land. And through that golden door our children can walk into tomorrow with the knowledge that no one can be denied the promise that is America.... In this springtime of hope, some lights seem eternal; America's is."

Although Abraham Lincoln led the nation during its darkest hours, he seemed to have an indomitable optimism about the nation's future. In his first inaugural address, he pled with his southern counterparts to avoid civil war. Near the end of the speech, he said;

I am loath to close. We are not enemies, but friends. We must not be enemies. Though passion may have strained, it must not break our bonds of affection. The mystic chords of memory, stretching from every battlefield and patriot grave to every living heart and hearthstone all over this broad land, will yet swell the chorus of the Union, when again touched, as surely they will be, by the better angels of our nature.

A LOOMING QUESTION

While Lincoln understood and often contemplated the dark side of human nature, his hope for a better future never seemed to dim. At his second inaugural, he said;

With malice toward none, with charity for all, with firmness in the right as God gives us to see the right, let us strive on to finish the work we are in, to bind up the nation's wounds, to care for him who shall have borne the battle and for his widow and his orphan, to do all which may achieve and cherish a just and lasting peace among ourselves and with all nations.

The optimism of Lincoln and Reagan was based on the good character of America's citizens. However, both recognized that citizens' character could change over time. They knew what we all know — what we teach our children from earliest days — that choices have consequences. And there was never a guarantee that America would always make good choices.

A question hangs over Lincoln's Gettysburg Address. Can a nation "conceived in Liberty, and dedicated to the proposition that all men are created equal… long endure?"

He ended with a thought that is both stirring and disquieting. "We here highly resolve that these dead shall not have died in vain — that this nation, under God, shall have a new birth of freedom — and that government of the people, by the people, for the people, shall not perish from the earth."

His words leave open the idea — obvious when you think about it — that such a government can "perish from the earth."

"O BEAUTIFUL FOR HEROES PROVED"

I love my country, and grieve at the thought of her ongoing deterioration and possible demise.

Whether carried by Boy Scouts or the Veterans of Foreign Wars, I feel a thrill and shiver every time I see Old Glory pass by. Few things are as moving as a gathering of military veterans. Some young, some old — they proved their willingness to place their lives in mortal danger for a cause greater than themselves. Many came away from war with physical or emotional wounds too great to be healed by modern science. Many of their companions did not return at all.

United States soldiers, sailors, airmen, and Marines fought for the rights and dignity of all Americans, and their efforts bore fruit far beyond our borders. They fought for ideals rooted in the character of God and His love of humanity.

For the most part, American wars have been altruistic. The nation fought in defense of freedom for itself and others — not conquest. That is why being defeated by the United States has usually been a blessing for America's foes. After World War II, Germany, Italy, and Japan became better, freer, more prosperous nations. They were enriched by the generosity of spirit found in those who vanquished them.

"TO THE EDGE OF DOOM"

Every year, the National Park Service hosts an event in Hawaii honoring Pearl Harbor survivors. The sad thing now is that we have so few left, and of course, the number goes down each year. I remember seeing a television story on the event and hearing a person at the podium saying something like this. "Now, for all of you who are able, please rise for the singing of our national anthem."

"… you who are able.…"

So young and vibrant in 1941, time had taken from these survivors what the Japanese fleet could not. I thought of the 2,403 killed that day, the 1,178 wounded. In John 15:13, Jesus said, "Greater love has no one than this, than to lay down one's life for his friends."

They laid down their lives for me, and they never even met me. Now I write about their beloved country, and mine. I write that God's judgment is on America; that we stand at what Shakespeare called "the edge of doom."

The world remembers Jeremiah as the weeping prophet, and I understand. He loved his country, but it had turned from God. It was his job to tell them they were facing God's judgment.

America, too, has fallen under the judgment of God. It's not an easy message, but it's a true one. And I am compelled to say it.

"Gospel" means "good news." Those who know God have every reason to be full of hope and joy. That does not change. But we Americans must recognize that the nation we live in has turned away from the God who has blessed it so richly. And now it faces judgment.

AMERICAN EXCEPTIONALISM

That things are going wrong in the United States is not news to most Americans. For years, polls have consistently shown that most people in the U.S. see their country headed in the wrong direction. An *NBC/Wall Street Journal* poll from April of 2016, showed 70 percent of Americans saw their country as "off on the wrong track." A 2015 Bloomberg poll found that 72% of Americans believe the country's greatest days are behind it.

In July of 2016, a Gallup poll gave us even more stunning numbers. It found that only 17% of Americans were "satisfied with the way things are going in the U.S."[5] That was down from 29% the previous month. Admittedly, late June and early July of 2016 were weeks filled with bad news. Nevertheless, the volatility in the poll shows the general level of anxiety most Americans feel.

I write these words during the first year of a new presidency. But Americans still aren't happy about the general direction of the country. An August 2017, a Rasmussen

---

5. "Americans' Satisfaction With U.S. Drops Sharply," Gallup, July 21, 2016

26

poll found, "Thirty-six percent of likely U.S. voters now think the country is heading in the right direction."

Many Christians feel that Donald Trump's election amounts to a reprieve. But a reprieve that lasts will only come with national repentance from sin — something many previous leaders not only believed, but said publicly.

President Trump campaigned with the slogan, "Make America Great Again." His opponents argued that it was unpatriotic even to suggest that it had fallen from its former greatness. His election, however, means that a large portion of the American people believe it has.

Earlier I quoted an article from *The Atlantic* saying, "Recent research bears out the stereotype, confirming that Americans really are more hopeful about the future than their peers in other wealthy nations."

The article didn't stop there. It went on to say, "But it also suggests that American optimism may now be waning."[6]

There is hope for this nation, but not if we ignore the problem.

"American exceptionalism" exists only to the extent that Americans remain exceptional. We have no promise

6. "What Makes Americans So Optimistic?" by Jared Keller, *The Atlantic*, March 25, 2015

from God that we can behave in any manner, and remain exceptional. In fact, we have the same promises as any other nation — nothing more, if also nothing less.

Chapter 3

GOD'S JUDGMENT PAST

THE UNITED STATES HAS FALLEN under the judgment of God before.

Like the rest of the 18th century world, Americans were desperately racist during the time of the nation's founding. Many of the founders were so accustomed to this that they had become blind to it.

We all know that a bad smell can seem to disappear over time. Only it doesn't really disappear. It's still there. You can't smell it anymore because you're suffering from something called "olfactory fatigue."

When it involves evil, the Bible has another description for olfactory fatigue. 1 Timothy 4:2 says it is like having your "conscience seared with a hot iron."

We can become so saturated with a certain kind of evil that we don't notice it anymore. The sin still stinks, but we no longer smell it. God, however, doesn't count that as an excuse. He sees our choices. He knows we have the capacity to remain sensitive to His standards of right and wrong. He's the One who put that capacity within us.

SLAVERY

Our nation's founders were amazing people, but they enshrined the wicked hypocrisy of slavery into the Constitution itself. That would turn out to be more than just a moral failure.

Slavery officially ended with passage of the Thirteenth Amendment to the Constitution. The Emancipation Proclamation foreshadowed that amendment. Other things prefigured it as well. In the long view of history, the Constitution's first ten amendments, collectively known as the Bill of Rights, seem to have doomed the institution from the beginning. Slavery was an affront to the spirit of those rights, and directly violates Amendments 1, 2, 4, 5, 6, and 8. We also see portents of slavery's demise in the Declaration of Independence, and the words, "All men are created equal."

Slavery's end finally goes back to the foundation of our understanding of the rights and dignity of humanity — to the Bible and its account of human creation in the image of God.

"So God created man in His own image; in the image of God He created him; male and female He created them." — Genesis 1:27.

THE "WOE DUE"

Many Americans, including President Lincoln, believed that the horrors of the Civil War were God's judgment for the sin of slavery. In his second inaugural address, he said;

> The Almighty has His own purposes. "Woe unto the world because of offenses; for it must needs be that offenses come, but woe to that man by whom the offense cometh."[1] If we shall suppose that American slavery is one of those offenses which, in the providence of God, must needs come, but which, having continued through His appointed time, He now wills to remove, and that He gives to both North and South this terrible war as the woe due to those by whom the offense came, shall we discern therein any departure from those divine attributes which the believers in a living God always ascribe to Him?
>
> Fondly do we hope, fervently do we pray, that this mighty scourge of war may speedily pass

1. Matthew 18:7

away. Yet, if God wills that it continue until all
the wealth piled by the bondsman's two hundred and fifty years of unrequited toil shall be
sunk, and until every drop of blood drawn with
the lash shall be paid by another drawn with
the sword, as was said three thousand years
ago, so still it must be said "the judgments of
the Lord are true and righteous altogether."[2]

In 1859, Lincoln wrote a letter to Henry L. Pearce sug-
gesting that God would judge America for the sin of slavery. "This is a world of compensations; and he who would
be no slave, must consent to have no slave. Those who
deny freedom to others, deserve it not for themselves; and,
under a just God, cannot long retain it."

More Americans died during the Civil War than
in the first two world wars combined. Somewhere
between 700,000 and 900,000 Americans lost their
lives in the fight between North and South. Eight percent of white males from 13 to 43 years old died in the
war. That number climbs to 18% when just looking at
the Confederacy. Among veterans of the war, one in 13
were left as amputees.

---

2. Psalm 19:9

GOD'S JUDGMENT

Does God really pour out His judgment on nations? Ask Sodom, Egypt, or Babylon. Ask the people of earth from Noah's day.

Was His judgment reserved exclusively for the Old Testament? No. Jesus pointed to judgments that fell on the earth in the time of Noah, and on Sodom during the days of Lot. He said these are examples of a judgment yet to come.[3]

When He sent out His disciples to preach, He said that those people and places that reject God's word should expect to be judged harshly. "Whoever will not receive you nor hear your words, when you depart from that house or city, shake off the dust from your feet. Assuredly, I say to you, it will be more tolerable for the land of Sodom and Gomorrah in the day of judgment than for that city!"[4]

The second half of the first chapter of Romans is all about God's judgment. We can see the reasoning behind His judgments in the sentences He pronounces. He gives them over to the very things they have chosen in place of

---

3. Luke 17:26-30
4. Matthew 10:14-15

Him — "the lusts of their hearts"[5] ... "vile passions"[6] ... "receiving in themselves the penalty of their error."[7]

Verse 28 says, "They did not like to retain God in their knowledge." They did not want God in their minds. So, He gave them what they wanted. The verse concludes, "God gave them over to a reprobate mind."[8]

He pours out His wrath on the unrighteous by letting their own desires overwhelm them. Verses 29 through 32 say, "Being filled with all unrighteousness, sexual immorality, wickedness, covetousness, maliciousness; full of envy, murder, strife, deceit, evil-mindedness; they are whisperers, backbiters, haters of God, violent, proud, boasters, inventors of evil things, disobedient to parents, undiscerning, untrustworthy, unloving, unforgiving, unmerciful; who, knowing the righteous judgment of God, that those who practice such things are deserving of death, not only do the same but also approve of those who practice them."

That is a picture of judgment, and it is also a picture of the United States of America in the twenty-first century. It's here now!

---

5. Romans 1:24
6. Romans 1:26
7. Romans 1:27
8. Romans 1:28 KJV

THANKSGIVING AND REPENTANCE

The first U.S. presidential Thanksgiving proclamation came from George Washington in the fall of 1789, just a few months after his inauguration in April. The proclamation wasn't just about giving thanks. It was also about repentance before God.

It began by saying, "It is the duty of all nations to acknowledge the providence of Almighty God, to obey His will, to be grateful for His benefits, and humbly to implore His protection and favor."[9]

According to Washington, it is our duty, not just to give thanks to God, but also "to obey His will."

After enumerating reasons for thankfulness, the proclamation called for a recognition of sin on a national level, and a humble cry for forgiveness. "And also that we may then unite in most humbly offering our prayers and supplications to the great Lord and Ruler of Nations and beseech Him to pardon our national and other transgressions."[10]

For what did they need to be forgiven? Plenty. In some ways, it was not so bad as today, but in other ways, it was worse. Here's the difference. As a nation. they approached God with humility. They recognized their shortcomings. And we do not.

---

9. George Washington, "Thanksgiving Proclamation of 1789"
10. Ibid.

Thanksgiving did not become a federal holiday in the U.S. until 1863, during the Administration of Abraham Lincoln. His Thanksgiving proclamation included a well-considered list of things for which the nation should be thankful. Even during the Civil War, the vulnerable nation remained at peace with other countries, grew wealthier, had abundant harvests, and grew in population.

Lincoln then said, "No human counsel hath devised nor hath any mortal hand worked out these great things. They are the gracious gifts of the Most High God, who, while dealing with us in anger for our sins, hath nevertheless remembered mercy."[11]

Lincoln believed God was dealing with America "in anger for our sins." He believed the Civil War was God's judgment on the United States for the sin of slavery. He urged Americans, not only to give thanks, but to repent.

> I recommend to them that while offering up the ascriptions justly due to Him for such singular deliverances and blessings, they do also, with humble penitence for our national perverseness and disobedience, commend to His tender care all those who have become widows, orphans, mourners or sufferers in the lamentable civil

---

11. Abraham Lincoln, "Thanksgiving Proclamation of 1863"

strife in which we are unavoidably engaged, and fervently implore the interposition of the Almighty Hand to heal the wounds of the nation and to restore it as soon as may be consistent with the Divine purposes to the full enjoyment of peace, harmony, tranquility and Union.[12]

12   Ibid.

Chapter 4

WHY WOULD GOD JUDGE AMERICA?

GOD JUDGES BECAUSE HE IS JUST, and justice demands consequences for choices. When God created Adam and Eve in the Garden of Eden, He could have made automatons who would always obey Him. But He wanted something more than a robotic existence for humankind.

He wanted our lives to have meaning. He endowed humanity the ability to give and receive love. This allows us to receive love from Him and to give it. It allows us to receive love from one another, and to give it.

Love requires choice.

Humanity fell from what God made us to be, but not because of a failure in our design. Rather, humanity fell because of the most amazing feature of that design — choice.

NURTURE... NATURE... CHOICE

Psychologists and sociologists have long debated which has more impact on us — nurture or nature. Was your character foreordained by your DNA, or did it come mostly from the circumstances in which you were raised?

The Bible gives a profound answer. It says that we are more than the sum of our genetics and environment. Those things are important, but beyond them, we still have the ability to choose. It's not a question of nurture or nature, but of nurture, nature, and choice.

Choice, though, is not choice if it doesn't mean anything. If I choose hell, but go to heaven anyway, then the choice was not real. For a choice to have meaning, it must have consequences. It must lead somewhere.

God will judge America because this nation is making a conscious choice to turn away from goodness — that is, from Him. And the path away from goodness always goes toward evil. God draws a line and says, "This side of the line is good." If you cross to the other side, you cross into the realm of evil.

In a democracy, choice is both a strength and a weakness. John Adams spoke of choice when he said: "We have no government... capable of contending with the human passions unbridled by morality and religion. Avarice, ambition, revenge and licentiousness would break the strongest cords of our Constitution, as a whale goes right through a net."

One generation takes a few steps away from God, and the next embraces levels of wickedness the first never dreamed possible. While atheists often do praiseworthy things, the idea that a people can maintain a broad spectrum of goodness over the long term without God is a fallacy. When America turned away from God, it turned to evil. While we already see results from this choice, those results will grow increasingly severe if we do not repent — that is, turn back to Him.

DISPOSABLE CHILDREN

God will judge America... for treating children as disposable.

Sexual permissiveness and perversions are destroying families. Is God against sex? No. He invented it. Sex is powerful, and if used as He directs, it is a tremendous force for good. It creates and strengthens families. But used in ways outside His will, its power becomes destructive. God made rules for our benefit. Misuse of the force we call sex, hurts everyone — especially children.

Want to see God's anger? Hurt the kids. In Matthew 18:6, Jesus said, "Whoever causes one of these little ones

41

who believe in Me to sin, it would be better for him if a millstone were hung around his neck, and he were drowned in the depth of the sea."

Believe me, that's not a level of wrath you ever want to see.

Jesus went on to say in verse 10, "Take heed that you do not despise one of these little ones, for I say to you that in heaven their angels always see the face of My Father who is in heaven."

Imagine a disaster completely wiping out the populations of some of America's largest cities. Let's say the disaster killed everyone in New York, Los Angeles, Chicago, Houston, Philadelphia, Phoenix, San Antonio, San Diego, Dallas, San Jose, Austin, Jacksonville, San Francisco, Indianapolis, Columbus, Detroit, and Seattle.

That's a lot of people, but it's only half the number of individuals killed by abortion in the United States since the Supreme Court legalized it in 1973. Jesus said not to despise the little ones, but we've violently destroyed fifty-nine million babies in just a few decades. What is that, if not despising the little ones?

AN ASIDE ON ABORTION

I should pause here in my countdown of America's guilt before God. I need to pause because I recognize that I may have just poured salt in a thousand wounds. If you've had an abortion, then I may have made you terribly uncomfortable. That is not my intention, and I hope you can forgive me.

Susan Estrich is a famous attorney and the former campaign manager for the 1988 Democratic nominee for President, Michael Dukakis. While she and I differ on all kinds of ideas, I've always admired her quick mind and thoughtfulness.

In 2005, several prominent women wore T-shirts in public venues that read, "I had an abortion." Planned Parenthood sold hundreds of them. I remember seeing Susan Estrich talk about abortion while wearing her T-shirt on a television program. She talked about the difficulty of that decision for her, and for most women who choose abortion.

Fiercely pro-choice, she wanted to stand with those women by wearing the shirt. Notice that I said, "pro-choice," and not "pro-abortion." They often amount to the same thing, but Ms. Estrich and others see an important distinction. I believe she would say she is not in favor of abortion. She favors a woman's right to choose abortion.

I'm inclined to believe her because I remember the look in her eye as she spoke about her own experience.

She would probably not call the emotion regret. But she showed unmistakable sadness as she wore her T-shirt and talked about her anguish in making that choice. She felt bullied by pro-life people she thought didn't understand. The discussion renewed her pain.

Abortion advocates invariably speak of abortion as a difficult choice. Why is it difficult? Why does the memory hurt? It hurts because Susan Estrich and women like her do not have hearts of stone. They know that in every abortion procedure, someone dies.

If you want to, go ahead and call that someone a "fetus" or "zygote." Those words deal with stages of development just like the words "adolescent" or "infant." When we speak of an aborted fetus, we're speaking of life — and not just any life. Human life.

So of course, it hurts when the topic comes up. But if you have accepted Christ's forgiveness for your sins, understand that He forgave them all. When He died on the cross, you had not been born. All your sins were still in the future. All of them. Those are the sins He died for.

Maybe you trust God's forgiveness, but still feel pain and regret when you think of the lost life of a child you never knew. Today, you can rest fully in the lavish, superabundant, utterly cleansing forgiveness of God through Christ.

And someday, you will meet that child, and you will know his or her forgiveness as well.

ABUSE OF THE VULNERABLE

<u>God will judge America</u>... for its treatment of the poor.

For some reading this book, the idea that God would judge the nation for its treatment of the poor makes no sense. You know that America spends vast sums of money every year on the poor. You wonder what more it can do.

You want the poor to stop doing the things that hurt themselves, and start doing things that will help. Bad choices can make people poor. I'm not exonerating people for the actions and attitudes they have chosen. My concern is with a society that encourages those actions and attitudes.

Deuteronomy 24:14 says, "You shall not oppress a hired servant who is poor and needy, whether one of your brethren or one of the aliens who is in your land within your gates."

Lyndon Johnson started a "war on poverty" in January of 1964. Yet today, the cycle of poverty is more severe and harder to escape than ever. Lobbyists craft laws supposedly meant to help the poor. But, too often, they write those laws in ways that will most benefit their clients — the rich.

Government "safety net" programs often use the poor merely as a pipeline for getting money into the pockets of the already wealthy.

Materialistic desires strike the poor as powerfully as they do the rich, but the poor must borrow to acquire the goods marketed to them. They are encouraged to go deeply into debt, often paying interest rates that would make a loan shark blush. Tennessee Ernie Ford sang, "Saint Peter, don't you call me 'cause I can't go. I owe my soul to the company store."[1]

It helps certain politicians to keep people beholden to government programs. To them, the poor mean votes. Most people want to end poverty, or at least make its symptoms less devastating and less permanent. But government programs too often do just the opposite. They can be bloated, ineffective, and ill-managed — their true benefits difficult to track.

Whether by mistake or design, government tends to enslave whole families in a cycle of ongoing poverty. It creates a victim mentality. And, even if you really are a victim, making that your focus will devastate your prospects for success. Politicians seem more interested in the votes of the poor than in helping to create paths out of poverty.

---

1. "Sixteen Tons" by Merle Travis, Warner/Chappell Music, Inc., 1946

I'm not saying to junk America's social safety net. I'm saying to make it work for the benefit of the poor, and not as a way to keep them down. Exploitation of the poor seems easy. Their poverty makes them vulnerable. But God watches over them.

Sometimes we say, "It's their own fault," and sometimes it is. But even then, God tells us they are precious to Him. Proverbs 14:31 says, "He who oppresses the poor reproaches his Maker."

You could say that other nations have been worse in their dealings with the poor, and you'd be right. But no other nation was ever blessed like the American nation. I started this book with a Bible verse that applies here. In Luke 12:48, Jesus said, "For everyone to whom much is given, from him much will be required."

REMOVING THE MORAL FOUNDATION

<u>God will judge America</u>... for removing His standards of right and wrong.

Proverbs 22:28 admonishes us, "Do not remove the ancient landmark Which your fathers have set."

Another way we hurt the little ones is to teach them that right and wrong are merely opinions. This removes the spiritual, social, and psychological foundations of their lives. The nation sows confusion in its young, and reaps their destruction. We've made them like pilots flying blind in a massive storm on a moonless night with complete instrument failure. In some cases, they don't even know up from down.

It's another way of teaching that God doesn't exist, or that, if He is real, then He doesn't care enough to communicate. It is a slap in His face, and utterly destructive to the next generation.

PORNOGRAPHIC AMERICA

<u>God will judge America</u>... for protecting the evil that destroys our young.

Citing frequent "incidents of sexual exploitation and violence," Cordelia Anderson, writing for Prevent Child Abuse Minnesota, called our society, "sexually toxic." She said, "Mass media is filled with 'pornified' images that pair sex with violence."[2]

She lamented the "normalization" of pornographic content and its availability to children. She wrote, "Normalization is the process by which an idea or behavior becomes an accepted part of societal culture.

---

2. PreventionWorks, the newsletter of Prevent Child Abuse Minnesota, Spring 2008

Once this happens, it is considered 'just the way it is,' 'just what people do,' and 'no big deal.'"[3]

She wrote that in 2008. Her fears turn out to have been well-founded. "Once barriers are removed," she wrote, "behaviors that once were recognized or perceived as being harmful, degrading, or deviant become viewed as beneficial or preferential and then beyond question."[4]

Since she wrote that, the process of "normalization" has turned children's access to pornography from a concern to a joke. In films and on television, boys as young as ten are depicted as rabid consumers of porn. It's made to seem normal — even funny. It has become a common source of jokes. In just a few years, it is already "beyond question."

People who show concern are reminded of an earlier era when boys found an adults stash of *Playboy Magazines*. Those magazines were far from innocent. But they were nothing like what's so easily available today. *Playboy* did not show full frontal nudity until the 1970s. On their phones, computers, or "smart TVs," today's young are a click away from levels of debauchery that would have resulted in jail sentences for their creators just a few years ago.

---

3. ibid.
4. ibid.

A single pornographic site contains almost 400,000 stories in English alone. One story on the site has been read almost 10 million times. Remember that sin is progressive. By nature, it waxes worse and worse. As a result, these are not just simple stories of sex. Incest stories are by far the most commonly written, and read. The top nine most read stories, and 36 of the top 50, are in that category. Some of the other categories on the site are not even printable. And this is just one of who knows how many pornographic websites, easily accessible regardless of age.

What is this doing to American minds and souls — no matter the age, but especially to the young? As destructive as stories can be, readily available visuals are even worse. They are depraved, violent, and demeaning to women as well as to men. They distort and degrade sexuality in general. And, once seen, they can't be unseen.

It's natural for children to feel curious. What's not natural, and is completely new in human history, is the easy access children now have to these images.

Kay Warren's husband, Rick, is one of the most influential Christians in the world. By 2007, his book, *The Purpose Driven Life* had sold over 30 million copies, most of them in hardback.

In books and articles, Kay has courageously helped thousands of women and men struggling with pornography. She helps by candidly speaking of her own struggle. As a small child, a church janitor's son molested her. But the little girl didn't tell a soul. She held it as a secret until she married. When she told Rick, she showed no emotion. To her young husband, the lack of emotion meant it was something she had already fully dealt with. He basically forgot it. But she didn't.

A victim's guilt is false and irrational. It has no basis in fact. But it is real in the victim's mind, and it doesn't go away by itself.

As a young teenager, while babysitting, Kay came across a collection of pornography. She wrote, "One night I picked it up and looked at it. Instant self-loathing, guilt, and remorse. How can I look at pornography? I love Jesus! I want to be a missionary! I'll never look at it again, I told myself. And I didn't. Until the next time I babysat. And the time after that. And the time after that. And before long, I was hooked. The good girl who loved Jesus with all her heart had a secret fascination with pornography, and the shame about killed me. I couldn't reconcile my temptations and my faith; I was torn apart on the inside. Worst of all, I couldn't tell anyone about it."[5]

5. *Sacred Privilege* by Kay Warren, 2017. Published by Revell, a division of Baker Publishing Group.

What she called her "off-and-on pornography fascination" stayed with her well into adulthood, and combined with several other factors to almost destroy her marriage.

Her story illustrates five important points:

• One — This is not a problem afflicting males only. The numbers are worse for boys and men, but it afflicts girls and women as well.

• Two — The effects of it don't magically disappear with the coming of adulthood.

• Three — This hits inside the church as well as outside.

• Four — It damages children, and the damage can last a lifetime.

• Five — With help, it doesn't have to last a lifetime. Christians can get victory over it.

I advise anyone struggling in this area to ask for help. A trusted friend, pastor, or Christian counselor can be invaluable. Just make sure they really are trustworthy. Talk about it. To use the biblical term, "confess" — not to the whole church, but to someone. And then empower that someone to hold you accountable.

James 5:16 says, "Therefore, confess your sins to one another, and pray for one another, so that you may be healed."[6]

The society fails to see how damaging these materials are, or else it doesn't care. As I mentioned before, the little ones are precious to God. In scripture, mistreating them is often the trigger that brings down judgment.

And this society has chosen to protect pornographers at the expense of its children.

CHOOSING LOSTNESS

<u>God will judge America</u>... because we have displaced Him from the center of life.

People try centering their lives on nothing, but it never works. They put themselves at the center, and civilization begins to fall apart. So, they turn to the state, to government.

In *A Christian Manifesto*, minister and philosopher Francis Schaeffer wrote, "We must realize that the Reformation world view leads in the direction of government freedom. But the humanist world view with inevitable certainty leads in the direction of statism. This is so because humanists,

---

6. NASB

having no god, must put something at the center, and it is inevitably society, government, or the state."

The usual liberal-conservative divide does not affect this. The various sides may want the state to do different things. They may worship it in different ways. But this sin crosses all political lines.

One problem with a government-centered worldview is that people begin to be judged by their perceived value to the state. This inevitably leads to increased levels of discrimination against individuals.

The dismissal of God the Creator is the point at which the philosophical underpinning of the United States — the idea that "all men are *created* equal" — falls into the garbage bin of history.

BLOOD LUST

<u>God will judge America</u>... because of its romance with violence.

Genesis 6:5 tells us that in the days of Noah, "The Lord saw that the wickedness of man was great in the earth, and that every intent of the thoughts of his heart was only evil continually." Verse 11 says, "The earth also was corrupt before God, and the earth was filled with violence."

The people of Noah's day were consumed by evil thoughts and violence. In our society, we see a juxtaposition of thought and violence in the area we call entertainment.

• We are entertained by watching heads explode and hearts ripped out of bodies.

• We are entertained by hours and hours of first-person shooter games where the killing goes on and on deep into every night.

• We are entertained by human bodies laid out in murderous death in the vilest ways imaginable. I mean that literally. Motion picture and television writers spend much of their working lives imagining ever more hideous expositions of human violence.

• A surprising amount of popular music glorifies violence of all kinds, but especially violence against women.

• Pornography is built on a foundation of violence against women.

• Even in sports, we long for the big hit, the fight, or the car crash with lots of fire and blood. When TV sportscasts show game highlights, they often choose what should be called lowlights.

- Our film and television heroes, when provoked even to small degrees, tend to respond by hitting or shooting.

In the next chapter, we will continue this sad journey to judgment.

Chapter 5

GOD WILL JUDGE AMERICA?

DURING WAR, WE PRAY. Afterwards, we brag.

During drought, we pray. Afterwards, we congratulate ourselves on our agricultural knowledge and methods.

During economic downturns, we pray. Afterwards, we strut our stuff.

When we perceive that we need Him, God becomes our go-to Big Guy. Afterwards, we barely give Him a thought.

Those things, and many others, illustrate our arrogance — pride.

THE PRIDE OF LIFE

God will judge America… because of her hubris.

In the book of Revelation, Jesus sent messages to seven churches in Asia Minor. America is obviously not one of those churches. But what the Lord said to the church at Laodicea brings America to mind.

> You say, 'I am rich, have become wealthy, and have need of nothing' — and do not know that you are wretched, miserable, poor, blind, and naked — I counsel you to buy from Me gold refined in the fire, that you may be rich; and white garments, that you may be clothed, that the shame of your nakedness may not be revealed; and anoint your eyes with eye salve, that you may see. As many as I love, I rebuke and chasten. Therefore be zealous and repent. Behold, I stand at the door and knock. If anyone hears My voice and opens the door, I will come in to him and dine with him, and he with Me.
> — Revelation 3:17-20

Like the people of that church from so long ago, affluence blinds America to her state of neediness.

In 2013, the term "affluenza" broke into the national consciousness. A Texas teenager, Ethan Couch, was on trial for manslaughter. He drove a pickup he had taken from his father without permission. He drove with more than three times the legal blood alcohol limit (at least partly from beer he had stolen) and while under the influence of valium and marijuana. Driving 70-mph in a

40-mph zone, he struck another vehicle. Four people died and nine were injured — one with complete paralysis.

His defense team called an expert witness, G. Dick Miller. He testified that Couch's problems were a result of "profoundly dysfunctional" parents. They had supposedly given Couch everything he wanted. He never learned accountability or the consequences of his actions.

The psychologist used the term "affluenza" to describe Couch's condition. You will not find the term defining a specific malady in medical textbooks or journals. But in pop culture, the word had traction. Most people did not see it as a legitimate defense in the Couch case, but everyone understood what it meant.

In America, our affluence has sickened us — knocked us out of balance, made us less than we should or could be.

"MY PEOPLE... CALLED BY MY NAME"

God will judge America... because of a backslidden and sinful church.

Much of the American church has become cold, indifferent, self-righteous, unloving, and unkind. But worst of all, it has compromised the Gospel. Some churches dilute the Good News with so much nonsense it becomes almost unrecognizable. Others have abandoned the Gospel altogether.

Don't misunderstand. Many magnificent churches remain in the land — their lights shining brighter than ever. If you're in one of them, don't be discouraged. You're not alone. But, in general, several deadly diseases have crept into America's pulpits, pews, Sunday School classes, small groups, seminaries, and, in some cases, even our times of worship.

I'm not talking about style. If someone from the 1950s could time travel to a Sunday morning worship service where I pastor — 412 Church in San Jacinto, California — they would suffer severe culture shock. The music is loud. The dress is casual. My style in the pulpit is anything but formal or stentorian. Our time-traveling evangelical would find the style surprising, but the message completely familiar.

Times change. Fashions change. The Gospel of Jesus does not change.

In 2014, then Secretary of State John Kerry made a speech that reflects a great deal of modern thought on the Bible's message. "Some people believe that people ought to… live by their interpretation of something that was written down… two thousand years ago. That's not the way I think most people want to live."

In other words, the two-thousand-year-old book known as the Bible is old, worn out, and hopelessly out of date.

A lot of people believe that. Others feel that Jesus was ahead of His time, but that the Bible is generally antiquated.

Jesus wasn't just ahead of His time. He was above time. His message and the message of His book are timeless. Everything else can change, but not God or His word. In Matthew 24:35, Jesus said, "Heaven and earth will pass away, but My words will by no means pass away."

The timeless, eternal quality of Christ results in a message that is also timeless and eternal. It is always relevant.

But some churches doubt His infinite relevance, and pitifully try to make themselves "relevant" by trying to seem more like the people of the world. They alter the Gospel to accommodate the moral fashions of our time. They disregard biblical truth and replace it with political correctness. But they're shooting at an ever-moving target. The best way to be relevant is to speak eternal, unchanging truths.

FILLED WITH BLOOD

It's natural to want others to like us. No one wants to be considered a "hater." No one wants to be looked down on as "one of those people." We want to be liked. We want to stand out for being great, not weird. And for the 21st century American church, more and more, the blood of Christ seems weird.

A fifth season episode of *The Andy Griffith Show*[1] begins with Andy and Barney working with files, and humming an old hymn. They briefly stop, talk about the work they're doing, then start to hum again — with Barney humming harmony.

Barney pauses his work for a few seconds, lost in the beauty of the melody. Then he turns to Andy and asks, "What's the name of that?"

Andy replies, "Sinners Lose All Their Guilty Stains.

In 1965, you might hear Granny on *The Beverly Hillbillies* sing "Throw Out the Lifeline." Or, someone might sing a hymn on a variety series. Such songs were not heard as frequently as they had been on fifties TV, but they were still on television.

It wasn't the Christian nature of Andy and Barney's song that made it so unique. It was the words of the song. Its name is "Praise for the Fountain Opened," but it's better known by its first line — "There is a Fountain Filled with Blood."

The first four lines say:

> *There is a fountain filled with blood*
> *Drawn from Immanuel's veins;*

---

1. *The Andy Griffith Show*, "The Case of the Punch in the Nose," directed by Coby Ruskin, written by Sam Bobrick and Bill Idelson, original airdate March 15, 1965.

And sinners, plunged beneath that flood,
Lose all their guilty stains.

It's not surprising that a television comedy would avoid lyrics about a fountain filled with blood. But why does it embarrass so many of today's churches?

1 Peter 1:18-19 says, "Knowing that you were not redeemed with corruptible things, like silver or gold… but with the precious blood of Christ."

In many American churches, you don't hear about the precious blood of Christ — not even during communion. In others, there are ceremonial mentions, but it's hidden under layers of tradition.

It makes sense that they would not feel a need to emphasize the blood of Christ. After all, Christ died for sinners. If a church doesn't talk about sin, there's no point in talking about redemption.

A MARKETABLE CHURCH

An interviewer pointed out to one prominent minister that he didn't "spend a lot of time in sermons talking about good and evil, sin and redemption." She asked, "Why don't you give people more of a moral template?"

AMERICA'S COMING JUDGMENT

He said that he does, but "in a positive way…. There's enough pushing people down in life already. When they come to my church, or our meetings, I want them to be lifted up. I want them to know that God's good."

The Andy Griffith Show at least mentioned "sinners," moral guilt, and redemption. But today, many churches fear that any mention of sin beats people up. They say people already feel bad about their sin, and they should not have to hear about it in church.

But that's exactly where they should hear about sin. In church, they can learn what to do about sin. That's because in church they can learn what God has done about it.

Today's leaders often want a marketable church. Sin and repentance seem anything but marketable. These leaders want a feel-good God and a happy religion — no unpleasantries. Does MacDonald's tell you you're a sinner? Does Apple? Much of the church now models itself after them.

Whether they intend to or not, thousands of American churches are selling out to the world. James 4:4 stands as a warning. "Do you not know that friendship with the world is enmity with God? Whoever therefore wants to be a friend of the world makes himself an enemy of God."

The message of the church has always triggered controversy. The Old Testament prophets were far from popular. Early Christians risked their lives just naming the name of Jesus. People are dying for His name right now in some parts of the world. Here in America, few of us face physical peril for the name of Christ. But we do face ridicule and scorn — and many can't take it.

TRUE MORAL GUILT BEFORE GOD

Not talking about sin is a fundamental error. Look at Galatians 3:24. "Therefore the law was our tutor to bring us to Christ, that we might be justified by faith."

What did this tutor teach us in order to bring us to Christ? It taught us that we cannot save ourselves. We cannot be good enough. The law set a standard that, in all of history, only Jesus consistently met. The law proves conclusively — leaves absolutely no doubt — that we can't be good enough on our own. And that knowledge brings us to Christ.

There is a famous story about Francis Schaeffer. He was asked, "What would you do if you met a really modern man on a train and you just had an hour to talk to him about the gospel?"

He answered, "I would spend 45-50 minutes on the negative, to really show him his dilemma — that he is morally dead — then I'd take 10-15 minutes to preach the Gospel. I believe that much of our evangelistic and personal work today is not clear simply because we are too anxious to get to the answer without having a man realize the real cause of his sickness, which is true moral guilt (and not just psychological guilt feelings) in the presence of God."

Sadly, in a large number churches across America, no one bothers about "true moral guilt." They're only interested in helping people banish "psychological guilt feelings." The word "sin" has been eliminated from many 21st century pulpits. The message, "You're a sinner and need a Savior," has been replaced with a message of self-esteem, self-love, and self-help. Sadly, this is the case in thousands of churches, including evangelical ones.

When churches try to change the unchangeable Gospel to make it compatible with whatever values are currently in fashion, it always leads to destruction.

Through the prophet Jeremiah, God laid out a situation similar to our own. Then He asked a profound question. "An astonishing and horrible thing Has been committed in the land: The prophets prophesy falsely, And the priests rule by their own power; And My people love to have it so. But what will you do in the end?"[2]

---

2. Jeremiah 5:30-31

TO AVOID JUDGMENT... PREACH JUDGMENT

The list of our national sins is long, and I won't continue to name them. These are enough.

When Jonah went to Nineveh, he gave a hard, hopeless message of coming judgment. The people repented, and God spared them.

Let's look again at words from Francis Schaeffer. In 1969, he wrote, "If He's really there and He's a holy God, do you seriously think that God does not care that a country like our own has turned from Him? There is only one kind of preaching that will do in a generation like ours — preaching which includes the preaching of the judgment of God."[3]

America has seen moral improvements since Schaeffer wrote those words in 1969. Those improvements should not be dismissed or belittled. But in the current climate, even the improvements are quickly being reversed. Outside the areas of improvement, we find vast wastelands where moral uprightness has been overwhelmed and destroyed by a sewer of evil.

The message of judgment is central to both the Old and New Testaments. No one can deny it without denying God's word.

---

3. *Death in the City* by Francis Schaeffer, InterVarsity Press, 1969

But our message of impending judgment is better than Jonah's. When we speak of judgment, we can tell our generation about God's ultimate act of judgment — the cross of Jesus. His ultimate act of judgment fell on Himself. He did nothing wrong, but took our sins on Himself. He received in Himself His own wrath and judgment against sin. That's what the cross means, and that's our hope.

Chapter 6

A PROPHET RISES

To UNDERSTAND THE GRAVITY of the danger facing America, we can look at a man who lived more than two and a half millennia ago. The man was a farmer, breeder of sheep, master shepherd… and then God made him a prophet.

He lived in the southern part of a divided land. The kingdoms were known as Judah in the south, with Jerusalem as its capital, and Israel in the north. At one time, it had all been Israel. But during the reign of Solomon's son Rehoboam, a tax dispute split it in two.

Both kingdoms repeatedly broke their covenant with God. The northern kingdom was especially bad. Idolatry there knew no bounds. To modern ears, people worshiping idols may sound harmless. But sin never sits still. It got so bad that to appease their pagan gods, these people began to place some of their own babies into sacrificial fires.

Seeing this, God sent prophets to warn them of their imminent danger. It became an era of prophets in the land of prophets. Their messages were unique and served various purposes, but all warned of God's impending judgment.

AMOS

Into this environment, the breeder of sheep arose with a message from God. His name was Amos. He was not a man of renown. He was not the son of a prophet. He had no particular pedigree. Until God gave him a specific call, he had simply tended his fields and flocks. He was not a gentleman-farmer, but a man with calloused hands and dirt under his fingernails.

People still say, "I'm just a poor" this or that. "I'm uneducated. I have no credentials. I'm from a small town." Some say, "I'm one small person in a huge city," "I'm too old," or "I'm too young."

Never think that because you lack status or prestige, God can't use you. Amos was a shepherd and a farmer from a small town outside Jerusalem. But God made him a prophet. His name and words have resounded across two and a half millennia. God can use every single person who is willing to say, "Here am I, send me."[1]

---

1. Isaiah 6:8

THE PRAYER OF AMOS

The kingdom was split, and so were the people. Those in the elite class had money and every advantage that comes with it. The lower classes merely made do. By the time of Amos, corrupt politicians, corrupt judges, and even corrupt religious leaders, had essentially wiped out the middle classes. This was already Israel's state when God sent the prophet Amos.

Amos 7:1-2 says, "Thus the Lord God showed me: Behold, He formed locust swarms at the beginning of the late crop; indeed it was the late crop after the king's mowings. And so it was, when they had finished eating the grass of the land, that I said: 'O Lord God, forgive, I pray! Oh, that Jacob may stand, For he is small!'"

God had given Isaac's son, Jacob, the name Israel at a key moment in the patriarch's adult life. So, by using the name Jacob, Amos was praying for the nation of Israel, but evoking the imagery of a young and vulnerable people. It may also be a recognition of Israel's unregenerate state at that time. It evokes the patriarch's name before God assigned him a new one, which signified rebirth.

To Amos, the swarms of locusts were an obvious representation of God's coming judgment. They meant famine and death. Amos said, "Oh, that Jacob may stand, For he is small!"

After Amos interceded with earnest prayer, God answered in Amos 7:3. "So the Lord relented concerning this. 'It shall not be,' said the Lord."

God tells us to pray. Philippians 4:6 says, "Be anxious for nothing, but in everything by prayer and supplication, with thanksgiving, let your requests be made known to God." The New Living Translation says it beautifully and simply. "Don't worry about anything; instead, pray about everything."[2]

He commands us to make our requests known. He doesn't always answer by saying, "Yes," as He did here. But He tells us to pray always.

Then God revealed more to Amos. "Thus the Lord God showed me: Behold, the Lord God called for conflict by fire, and it consumed the great deep and devoured the territory."[3]

After this vision, Amos again pled his case to God. "'O Lord God, cease, I pray! Oh, that Jacob may stand, For he is small!' So the Lord relented concerning this. 'This also shall not be,' said the Lord God."[4]

Amos again interceded for his people, and God again relented.

---

2. Philippians 4:6 NLT
3. Amos 7:4
4. Amos 7:5-6

PLUMB LINE

Then the Lord showed Amos something that could not be so easily dismissed.

"Thus He showed me: Behold, the Lord stood on a wall made with a plumb line, with a plumb line in His hand. And the Lord said to me, 'Amos, what do you see?' And I said, 'A plumb line.' Then the Lord said: 'Behold, I am setting a plumb line In the midst of My people Israel; I will not pass by them anymore. The high places of Isaac shall be desolate.'"[5]

Verse 7 of chapter 7 says, "Behold, the Lord stood on a wall made with a plumb line." That means a wall perfectly perpendicular, perfectly straight. The plumb line in the Lord's hand is a tool for measuring uprightness.

In verse 8, the Lord asks, "Amos, what do you see?" Amos said, "A plumb line."

Men have used this device since the master builders of ancient Egypt. Today's construction engineers use tools that still operate on the same principle. The device itself is amazingly simple — a string with a weight at the end. The weight is known as a "plumb bob."

You hold the string up, allowing the weighted end at the bottom to hang free. When it stops moving, you have a

---

5. Amos 7:7-9

line perfectly perpendicular to the earth's center of gravity. If you want to build a wall, you want it to be "plumb," meaning perfectly straight — not perpendicular to the uneven ground, but aligned to the planet itself.

As an absolute standard by which to measure, the plumb line represents the word of God. When God founded the nation, He laid out laws to direct their lives, and the life of the nation. He founded Israel on His word. To be aligned with the perfect morality of God Himself, we must use the plumb line of His word.

Verse 8 continues, "Then the Lord said: 'Behold, I am setting a plumb line In the midst of My people Israel; I will not pass by them anymore. The high places of Isaac shall be desolate.'"[6]

Game over. Judgment is here!

God holds a plumb line — His word. He measures all human activity against this line, but that's especially true of Israel because He gave His word specifically to them. And Israel was not plumb. It was no longer aligned to the word God had given. Instead of straight up and down, the wall was angled, bent, crooked.

---

6. Amos 7:8-9

ISRAEL ASKEW

Exodus 19:7 says, "So Moses came and called for the elders of the people, and laid before them all these words which the Lord commanded him."

Moses laid out the words of God's covenant with the people of Israel. It was a two-way contract. In Exodus 19:8, the nation, in effect, shook hands with God on the deal. "Then all the people answered together and said, 'All that the Lord has spoken we will do.' So Moses brought back the words of the people to the Lord."

The covenant became the plumb line.

Moses is saying, in effect, "Lord, all of the people saw Your plumb line. They heard Your word, and agreed to Your terms. They will carry out their end of the bargain. They said, 'We will do it.'"

They reiterated their agreement to these terms in Exodus 24:7. Moses "took the Book of the Covenant and read in the hearing of the people. And they said, 'All that the Lord has said we will do, and be obedient.'"

The plumb line of Amos 7 is the Word of the Lord, to which the people in their contract agreed, but failed to keep.

In Amos 7:9, God began to pronounce judgment — not so much on specific individuals here, but on the nation.

He said He would lay waste to the high places of Isaac and make them desolate. "High places" meant the hilltop shrines dedicated to idols.

Even the once holy sanctuaries, had become false. God would destroy them, also. As for the king, He said, "I will rise with the sword against the house of Jeroboam." Their politics had become evil, and their government would fall.

As a people, they had covenanted with God saying, "All that the Lord has spoken we will do." That became the plumb line — "All that the Lord has spoken."

OODLES OF RELIGION

The people went to the temple and "did religion," but they did not repent. They went to "church," so to speak, but did not love God. They "had religion," but it did not connect with God. They were spiritual, but their spirituality was not in God. Israel no longer knew the God of its fathers.

In the time of Amos, temples were a central part of life in the northern kingdom. But those temples, instead of pleasing God, were built in direct defiance of His expressed will.

Deuteronomy 12:5 warns against this. It says, "You shall seek the place where the Lord your God chooses, out of all your tribes, to put His name for His dwelling place; and there you shall go."

That meant there would be a single place for worship and sacrifice, and it would be at a location chosen by God. As the children of Israel traveled 40 years through the wilderness, God always chose the location of the tabernacle. In the days of David, God chose the location on Mount Moriah (what we call the Temple Mount) where His one temple would stand.

The first ruler of the northern kingdom, King Jeroboam, feared that decree from God. He thought that if the people of his newly acquired kingdom went to God's one sanctioned place of worship and sacrifice — the Temple in Jerusalem — they might again look to the house of David for their rulers.

So, he decided to build temples in the north in direct defiance of God's will. As I said before, sin never stands still. Satan always wants more. Jeroboam soon made golden calves, and said to the people, "Here are your gods, O Israel."

CHOOSING IDOLATRY

Amos preached in the days of Jeroboam's namesake, the 14th ruler of the northern kingdom — Jeroboam the son of Joash. 2 Kings 14:24 says, "He did evil in the sight of the Lord."

For a while, things went swimmingly for Jeroboam II. He "restored the territory of Israel from the entrance of Hamath to the Sea of the Arabah."[7]

Nelson's Bible Dictionary says, "During this time of superficial prosperity, the prophet Amos especially spoke out against the many social abuses in Israel. A severe oppression of the poor had been instituted by the newly prosperous class. Justice was in the hands of lawless judges; dishonest merchants falsified the balances by deceit; and worship was little more than a pious smokescreen that covered the terrible abuses of the poor. Amos prophesied that the destructive fury of God would fall upon the house of Jeroboam."[8]

Under the first Jeroboam, Israel eschewed the "organized religion" of God's covenant given through Moses. None of the northern kingdom's kings would truly repent and destroy the golden gods because the idols gave people a sense of tradition and religiosity.

The most precious gift ever given to a nation was when the Lord of the universe spoke to Abraham, Isaac, Jacob,

---

7. 2 Kings 14:25
8. *Nelson's Illustrated Bible Dictionary*, Copyright © 1986, Thomas Nelson Publishers

and their progeny. But the people rejected God's revelation. Largely out of convenience and a desire to obtain and hold power, they chose the baser things of this world instead of the glory of Almighty God. They went to temple and worshiped their false gods, all the time sinning like the devil they now exalted.

God also gave America precious gifts. But today, vast portions of the population have chosen to pour contempt on those gifts.

Chapter 7

MORAL CERTAINTY

JUDGMENT, WRATH, ANGER... Americans rarely associate God with such words. But that was not always true.

C. S. Lewis wrote, "The ancient man approached God (or even the gods) as the accused person approaches his judge. For the modern man, the roles are quite reversed. He is the judge: God is in the dock."[1]

How many times have you heard someone say, "I could never believe in (or trust, or serve) a God Who...." You can fill in the rest with whatever point the speaker considers the God of the Bible to have failed. It might be "Who allows evil in the world" ... or, "Who condemns people for who they love" ... or, "Who would send anyone to hell."

---

1. *God in the Dock: Essays on Theology and Ethics*, by C. S. Lewis, edited by Walter Hooper, William B. Eerdmans Company, 1970

There are dozens, maybe thousands, more. Those who condemn God for His exhortations and prohibitions, fail to understand that all of them are for our good. His rules come from a heart of love, as well as justice.

Whether we understand all His motivations or not, we need to know that He is God, and we are not.

MORAL RELATIVISM

C. S. Lewis said something else that can be helpful here. In *Mere Christianity*, he pointed out that we all have moral standards of some kind and at some level. Even the most died-in-the-wool moral relativist will cry foul if you, for instance, steal his parking space.

> *"You stole my parking space!"*
>
> *"But I felt that it was okay for me to do that today."*
>
> *"Well, it's not okay."*
>
> *"Yes, but I am sincere in believing that for me it is okay."*
>
> *"Listen, buddy, you can do what you want to, but when you tread on my rights, you're wrong."*
>
> *"But I don't feel that I am wrong."*
>
> *"Your rights end at my parking space!"*
>
> *"And so does your moral relativism."*

When the moral relativist says, "You can do whatever you want as long as it doesn't hurt someone else," he ceases to be a moral relativist. Now he has become a moral absolutist. "As long as it doesn't hurt someone else" is a moral absolute. He may draw the line between right and wrong in a different place than someone else, but if the line exists, then there can be no moral relativism.

When anyone claims that his own values are more honorable than Hitler's — to use an extreme example — that person is claiming that some moral values are better than others. But the only way his values can be *better* than Hitler's is for his values to be closer to perfection than Hitler's. That, of course, means that a perfect set of values somewhere exists — an absolute moral standard.

But if we believe morality is a made-up human construction within an infinite emptiness, who can claim to be better than another? On the other hand, if some actions or words or thoughts are better than others, then an absolute plumb line must exist somewhere.

The problem is, who in all the universe has the right to calibrate such a plumb line? The answer is, of course, obvious. The Creator does.

A MORAL CERTAINTY

Hebrews 13:8 says, "Jesus Christ is the same yesterday, today, and forever."

Jesus said that His words are like a rock.[2] They do not change. They do not shift. They don't have to keep up with the times, because, like Him, they are above time.

Isaiah calls God "the High and Lofty One Who inhabits eternity."[3] The word translated "inhabits" comes from the Hebrew word, "shokeen." It refers to a place of lodging or residence. Where does God reside? Eternity.

Genesis 1:1 describes Him speaking the universe (including time) into existence. And we're going to tell Him that since we don't think He's up to snuff on twentieth century political correctness, that He must be immoral?

Does the painting cry out against the painter that the sunset should really be blue?

It all boils down to this. Is there a God? Does He care about morality? Has He revealed Himself and His moral standards to humanity?

---

2. Matthew 7:24-27
3. Isaiah 57:15

EVIDENCE OF GOD AND HIS CARE

Thousands of books have been written giving powerful evidence of God's existence. Thousands of books have been written showing that He has spoken through His prophets in the Bible.

But it's such a crucial point, let's look at one of the thousands of answers showing the veracity of the Bible's claims about God's identity. The answer starts with a question. Over the centuries, thousands have claimed to speak for God. Is there a way to verify that it is God who has spoken through a prophet? Can we know that he or she is not just a self-deluded individual or a liar?

If we can verify that God has spoken through the prophet, it tells us several important things. 1) God must exist. He can't speak if He is not there. 2) If He speaks on issues of human morality, then He must care about how we conduct ourselves. 3) If we could verify that He was the One speaking, we could know what He expects of us. From that, we would gain understanding of our meaning and purpose.

So, is there a way to verify that someone who claims to be a prophet does in fact speak for God? In Deuteronomy 18:22, God told Moses how to be certain the prophet was hearing from Him. Even if you don't accept the Bible as

God's word, you must admit that the method given makes a fair and reasonable way to judge the issue.

Deuteronomy 18:21-22 says, "And if you say in your heart, 'How shall we know the word which the Lord has not spoken?' — when a prophet speaks in the name of the Lord, if the thing does not happen or come to pass, that is the thing which the Lord has not spoken; the prophet has spoken it presumptuously; you shall not be afraid of him."

KLAATU'S EQUATION

Do you remember the old movie, "The Day the Earth Stood Still?"[4] There's a newer version, but I'm thinking of the one from 1951 directed by Robert Wise and starring Michael Rennie as the alien "Klaatu." The alien needs to leave a calling card that will convince a famous scientist of Klaatu's identity. He sees a formula on the scientist's chalkboard, and adds an equation to it that the scientist will recognize as coming from a higher intelligence.

God did something like that with the Bible. He left messages that only He could leave. He described events that would happen hours, days, years, or even centuries later. Like the fictional Klaatu, the real God left us a self-verifying message.

---

4. *The Day the Earth Stood Still*, directed by Robert Wise, screenplay by Edmund H. North based on a story by Harry Bates, 1951.

To know that it was Him, we look at what He foretold. If the message contained information that only God would know, we can surmise that it must have come from Him.

But the Bible has more than that. We should also ask if the messages were abundant enough and specific enough that it couldn't have been a series of lucky guesses. If so, then the information could have come only from a Being Who is above time and space. Only One Being makes that claim — God.

Here's another verse along the same lines. Jeremiah 28:9 says, "As for the prophet who prophesies of peace, when the word of the prophet comes to pass, the prophet will be known as one whom the Lord has truly sent."

Since none of us knows the future, true prophecy serves as powerful evidence of God's existence. It also gives us His standards of human conduct, and, ultimately, the meaning of our lives.

GOD ALWAYS AGREES WITH HIMSELF

There's another important thing about messages from God. If He said them, they will not contradict previous things He has said. That's why Deuteronomy 13:1-4 says;

> If there arises among you a prophet or a dreamer of dreams, and he gives you a sign or

a wonder, and the sign or the wonder comes to pass, of which he spoke to you, saying, 'Let us go after other gods' — which you have not known — 'and let us serve them,' you shall not listen to the words of that prophet or that dreamer of dreams, for the Lord your God is testing you to know whether you love the Lord your God with all your heart and with all your soul. You shall walk after the Lord your God and fear Him, and keep His commandments and obey His voice; you shall serve Him and hold fast to Him.

If a message is really from God, it will agree with previous messages from God. The Bible alone fits the bill, Famed Christian teacher Josh McDowell said;

Here was a book written over a period of one thousand five-hundred years. Forty something authors from every single walk of life — philosophers, fishermen, poets, statesmen, cupbearers, tax collectors. Written in different places — in the wilderness, dungeons, the palace, a military campaign. Written during times of war and times of peace. They wrote in different moods — some from the heights of joy, others from the depths of sorrow. Written on

three continents — Africa, Asia, and Europe....
And they wrote on hundreds of controversial
subjects... with harmony and continuity from
beginning to end.[5]

He defined as controversial any subject that immediately
evokes several different opinions. The truth is, very few
single authors remain consistent from book to book, or
even from chapter to chapter. The Bible, written by large
numbers of diverse human authors over a vast period
time and in different cultures, does.

EXCITING NEWS!

God is, and He has spoken.

The Old Testament is full of prophecies about Jesus. He
would be a descendant of Abraham, born to the house
of David. He would be born in Bethlehem, and, get
this, He would be born of a virgin. The Old Testament
describes His crucifixion in excruciating detail hundreds
of years before it happened. In fact, in His life, Jesus fulfilled well over 300 messianic prophecies. The miracle is
not just that Jesus fit the criteria, but that any man on
the face of the earth at any point in history, would fit
the criteria.

---

5. *A Ready Defense* by Josh McDowell, audio. 1993

But all that was a long time ago. What about today?

The present existence of the State of Israel and of the Jewish people stands as another reliable proof of God's existence and of His prophets' veracity. No other people dispersed around the world managed to stay intact more than a few generations, much less return to the land from which they had been expelled. The Bible said it would happen, and it's happening right now.

The Bible tells of technology that would come into existence in the end times — and for the first time in the history of the world, we now have much of that technology. The world monetary system every day looks more like the one prophesied in the Bible two thousand years ago. I could go on and on with examples of ancient prophecies being fulfilled now — in our generation.

Don't confuse this with Nostradamus-style vagueness. While some Bible prophecies are vague and difficult to understand, others are unmistakable.

How could anyone two or three thousand years ago, know so much about today? Because God spoke. That makes the Bible self-authenticating. If these men and women heard from God about future events, then we can also trust the statements regarding God's standards of morality. Prophecies and moral standards are utterly intertwined.

Chapter 8

FOUNDING FATHERS: WASHINGTON

WE LIVE IN A POST-CHRISTIAN ERA of American history. That does not mean that this was ever a "Christian nation." But it was governed under what Francis Schaeffer called "a Christian consensus."

The late great Tim LaHaye is famous for coauthoring the *Left Behind* series, but most of his work was nonfiction, including *Faith of Our Founding Fathers*. In that book, LaHaye wrote, "This Christian consensus is easily verified by the fact that prior to 1789 (the year that eleven of the thirteen states ratified the Constitution), many of the states still had constitutional requirements that a man must be a Christian in order to hold public office."[1]

---

1. *Faith of Our Founding Fathers* by Tim LaHaye, Wolgemuth & Hyatt Publishers, 1987

Such requirements did not make America a Christian nation, but they give evidence of a powerful Christian influence. The founders built America on a foundation of aspirations and standards gleaned from the Bible. In many ways, that made it a land built according to God's plumb line. I know that's not the popular opinion right now, but let's look at the evidence.

DEISTS?

We often hear that many, if not most, of the Founding Fathers were deists. *Merriam-Webster.com* defines deism as "a movement or system of thought advocating natural religion, emphasizing morality, and in the 18th century denying the interference of the Creator with the laws of the universe."

Dictionary.com gives two definitions. One — "belief in the existence of a God on the evidence of reason and nature only, with rejection of supernatural revelation." Two — "belief in a God who created the world but has since remained indifferent to it."

A deist believes God created the world, set it in operation, and then stepped aside. They believe God has not spoken, and gives no revelation. If such a God is interested in humanity, He never shows it. It was a common philosophy in the 1700s. And, yes, there were some deists among the founders. But not many.

In the Summer of 2016, on the television program *Outnumbered*, Fox News contributor Julie Roginsky gave the usual party line about the founding fathers. Dr. Sebastian Gorka was a guest on the program that day. He is the author of the book, *Defeating Jihad,* and would later become a deputy assistant to President Donald Trump.

He had just said, "We don't know where the refugees from war zones are living in America! We are a Christian nation. We should be charitable to those in need. But charity is not an excuse for suicide."

Let me say here that I disagree with the wording of Dr. Gorka's statement. As I saod earlier, we are not and have never been a "Christian nation" *per se*. Instead, I would say we are a nation whose founding principles were biblically-based.

Julie Roginsky is a woman of Jewish descent born in Moscow. Her parents were Soviet dissidents. She and her family came to the United States in 1980. Roginsky became an influential democratic media consultant.

She took issue with the statement, "We are a Christian nation."

She disagreed with it, but didn't really want to pursue it during her time to ask questions. So, she hit him with a quick jab before going to the point she really wanted to

AMERICA'S COMING JUDGMENT

make. She said, "Dr. Gorka, I'm going to put aside the 'Christian nation' part because I thought we didn't have a state religion, but that aside, I keep hearing about…."

But Gorka seemed determined not to let her go on until he could respond to her jab. He said, "That's not a statement about state religion."

Julie went ahead and asked her question, but her first comment still troubled Dr. Gorka. So, before answering the question, he said, "I can't drop that. The capital 'C' Creator in our founding document — who do you think the founding fathers were referring to? Allah? No. Jesus Christ."

To a Jewish woman raised by Soviet dissidents, this did not go over well. To fight back, she used a line being hammered into young people in schools across America. She said, "Well, sir, most of them were Deists. We could have a separate discussion about that, but…."

Gorka said, "Not true. Not true. That's conventional wisdom."

Then they went back to her question.

While the United States is not a Christian nation, it was most definitely founded primarily by Christians — not Deists — and on biblical principles.

FOUNDING FATHERS: WASHINGTON

CHRISTIANS!

University of Dallas professor M. E. Bradford reviewed the religious beliefs of the founders, concluding that, with only a few exceptions, Christian men wrote the U.S. Constitution. He said, "With no more than five exceptions... they were orthodox members of one of the established Christian communions: approximately twenty-nine Anglicans, sixteen to eighteen Calvinists, two Methodists, two Lutherans, two Roman Catholics, one lapsed Quaker and sometime Anglican, and one open Deist — Dr. Franklin who attended every kind of Christian worship, called for public prayer, and contributed to all denominations."

As we will see a little later, Benjamin Franklin did at times call himself a deist, but insisted that he was also a Christian. This one man hardly makes the case that, of the founding fathers, "most of them were Deists."

Dr. Bradford also said:

> Their total political experience at the state and national level is so great as to suggest that as a company they are a dependable barometer of American attitudes and beliefs at the close of the eighteenth century: in the important things resembling most of their countrymen but more

capable of making the necessary political dis-
criminations that would "preserve, protect,
defend" the common good.

In other words, they represented well the American
populace at that time in history.

WASHINGTON

George Washington was not a Deist. In a letter to
Thomas Nelson in 1778, he wrote, "The Hand of providence has been so conspicuous in all this, that he must
be worse than an infidel that lacks faith, and more than
wicked, that has not gratitude enough to acknowledge his
obligations."

Like others of his time, Washington modestly used the
term "providence" instead of saying God. In this way,
people of that era were like the Children of Israel who, in
order never to use God's holy name in vain, removed the
vowels so it could not be spoken. Using the word "providence" for God was, for most of them, an act of humility.

In any case, you can be sure that no Deist believes, "The
Hand of providence has been… conspicuous."

In the 1830s, writer and historian Jared Sparks searched
out and compiled a series of books called, *The Writings of
George Washington*. His work filled 12 volumes. He wrote,

"To say that he (Washington) was not a Christian would be to impeach his sincerity and honesty. Of all men in the world, Washington was certainly the last whom any one would charge with dissimulation or indirectness; and if he was so scrupulous in avoiding even a shadow of these faults in every known act of his life, however unimportant, is it likely, is it credible, that in a matter of the highest and most serious importance he should practice through a long series of years a deliberate deception upon his friends and the public? It is neither credible nor possible."

After the death of his stepson, Washington adopted his granddaughter, Nelly Parke Custis. She lived the first twenty years of her life at Mount Vernon. She knew Washington as a father. Nelly spoke movingly of his faith, his work in church, and of regular and disciplined morning and evening devotions.

When asked about his Christian faith, she said, "I should have thought it the greatest heresy to doubt his firm belief in Christianity. His life, his writings, prove that he was a Christian." She added, "He was not one of those who act or pray, 'that they may be seen of men.'"[2] She said that to question George Washington's faith in Christ would be as ridiculous as to question his patriotism.

---

2. She said this quoting Jesus talking about hypocrites in Matthew 6:5 and 23:5.

America's first President determined never to politicize or otherwise cheapen his faith. He was not always a humble man, but he was humble before God. This approach to Christianity made his faith extremely private, giving critics an opening. But those who knew him best saw him as a man of deep and abiding Christian faith.

Robert Lewis served as George Washington's secretary from 1789 to 1791. He was also Washington's nephew. In the book, *Washington's Writings*, author William White wrote, "Being a nephew of Washington, and his private secretary during the first part of his presidency, Mr. Lewis lived with him on terms of intimacy, and had the best opportunity for observing his habits. Mr. Lewis said that he had accidentally witnessed his private devotions in his library both morning and evening; that on those occasions he had seen him in a kneeling posture with a Bible open before him, and that he believed such to have been his daily practice.'"

This is consistent with the testimony of Nelly Parke Custis and others who knew him well.

Chapter 9

FOUNDING FATHERS: JEFFERSON, MADISON, FRANKLIN

THOSE WHO TRY TO MINIMIZE the influence of the Bible on the thinking of the founders often point to Thomas Jefferson. He served as the principal author of the Declaration of Independence, and later as the third President of the United States. Popular philosophies highly regarded in France at the time, strongly influenced Jefferson.

Though not an orthodox Christian, Jefferson described his own thinking as "very different from that anti-Christian system imputed to me by those who know nothing of my opinions." He did not believe in the deity of Jesus, but called the Lord's words, "The most sublime and benevolent code of morals which has ever been offered to man."[1]

We will look at it in more depth later, but for now, remember something I said earlier about the Declaration of Independence. It begins with a statement of faith.

Jefferson considered himself both a deist and a Christian. In *The Mosaic of Christian Belief*, Roger Olson wrote, "Other Deists and natural religionists who considered themselves Christians in some sense of the word included Thomas Jefferson and Benjamin Franklin."[2]

Although Jefferson rejected Christian orthodoxy, he highly esteemed the teachings of Christ. He took a Bible and physically cut out Jesus' words — what we might call the "red letters" — and pasted them into a separate book.

Jefferson was the outlier, one of only a tiny percentage who did not openly profess Christianity. Yet even he was a determined student of the Bible, and profoundly influenced by the teachings of Jesus.

MADISON

James Madison is considered the "Father of the Constitution." Senator William Cabell Rives wrote a

---

1. Letter to John Adams, October 12, 1813.
2. *The Mosaic of Christian Belief: Twenty Centuries of Unity & Diversity* by Roger E. Olson, Intervarsity Press. 2009

landmark three volume biography of Madison. He said, "After the manner of the Bereans, he seems to have searched the Scriptures daily and diligently.... He explored the whole history and evidences of Christianity on every side."[3]

Madison wrote:

> I have sometimes thought there could not be a stronger testimony in favor of religion or against temporal enjoyments, even the most rational and manly, than for men who occupy the most honorable and gainful departments and [who] are rising in reputation and wealth, publicly to declare their unsatisfactoriness by becoming fervent advocates in the cause of Christ.

And:

> [A] watchful eye must be kept on ourselves lest, while we are building ideal monuments of renown and bliss here, we neglect to have our names enrolled in the Annals of Heaven.

He wrote, "The belief in a God All Powerful wise & good, is so essential to the moral order of the World and to the happiness of man."

---

3. *History of the Life and Times of James Madison, Volume 1* by William Cabell Rives, published by Boston, Little, Brown and Company, 1868

We see the wisdom of those words confirmed before our eyes. As belief in God dwindles, moral order disintegrates. Madison, a student of scripture, saw it, too.

FRANKLIN

Other than Benjamin Franklin himself, few would characterize him as a Christian. Nevertheless, he respected God and the Bible. He understood that Someone had to be holding everything together, and the moment we turn away from that Someone, we get disaster.

Think about these words from his 1768 version of the Lord's Prayer. "Heavenly Father, may all revere thee, and become thy dutiful Children and faithful Subjects; may thy Laws be obeyed on Earth as perfectly as they are in Heaven."

That sounds like someone with respect for Jesus and the Bible.

He went on, "Provide for us this Day as thou hast hitherto daily done: Forgive us our Trespasses, and enable us likewise to forgive those that offend us. Keep us out of Temptation, and deliver us from Evil."

In 1782, Franklin wrote a pamphlet called, "Information to Those Who Would Remove to America." As the title suggests, he wrote it for Europeans considering a move to the new world. He wanted America to sound good, but also wanted to attract morally upright immigrants. For both purposes, he emphasized America's faith in God.

He wrote:

> Industry and constant Employment are great Preservatives of the Morals and Virtue of a Nation. Hence bad Examples to Youth are more rare in America, which must be a comfortable Consideration to Parents. To this may be truly added that serious Religion under its various Denominations is not only tolerated but respected and practiced. Atheism is unknown there, Infidelity rare & secret, so that Persons may live to a great Age in that Country without having their Piety shock'd by meeting with either an Atheist or an Infidel. And the Divine Being seems to have manifested his Approbation [approval] of the mutual Forbearance and Kindness with which the different Sects treat each other, by the remarkable Prosperity with which He has been pleased to favor the whole Country.

Later, at a moment when the long-term existence of the United States of America remained in doubt, the 82-year-old Franklin gave a message of faith that would change the world. It was July of 1787, and the Constitutional Convention seemed to be going nowhere. Some thought a new national government would never be born.

Others expected a Constitution that would destroy the rights fought for in the Revolutionary War. Patrick Henry turned down his invitation to attend. He later explained that it was because he "smelt a rat in Philadelphia, tending toward monarchy." It was a valid concern, and many felt as he did.

America didn't just face a fork in the road, but a full-blown freeway interchange with multiple possible outcomes. Would they be able to agree on key points? Would the weak Articles of Confederation continue in effect? Or, would they go too far the other direction, and make an intrusive, rights-stifling federal government? The shape of America's future rested in the balance.

The impasse finally grew so severe that it threatened the future of what de Tocqueville called "the great American experiment." "Government of the people, by the people, for the people" might have died before it was fully born.

Franklin, who had mostly been quiet during the proceedings, at last rose to address his fellow delegates.

> I have lived, Sir, a long time, and the longer
> I live, the more convincing proofs I see of

this truth — that God governs in the affairs of men. And if a sparrow cannot fall to the ground without His notice, is it probable that an empire can rise without His aid? We have been assured, Sir, in the sacred writings, that "except the Lord build the House they labor in vain that build it." I firmly believe this; and I also believe that without His concurring aid we shall succeed in this political building no better than the Builders of Babel.... I therefore beg leave to move that henceforth prayers imploring the assistance of Heaven, and its blessings on our deliberations, be held in this Assembly every morning before we proceed to business.

The supposed "deist" called for prayer, quoted Jesus, and acknowledged the necessity of God's blessing to make the United States a great nation. Consider Psalm 127:1 which he quoted. "Except the Lord build the house, they labour in vain that build it."[4]

That is a direct repudiation of deism. He followed those words by saying, "I firmly believe this." Deists do not believe in an interested God.

---

4. KJV

Franklin also referenced the words of Jesus in Matthew 10:29. "Are not two sparrows sold for a farthing? and one of them shall not fall on the ground without your Father."[5]

Nothing could be further from deism! Jesus went on to say, "But the very hairs of your head are all numbered. Fear ye not therefore, ye are of more value than many sparrows."[6]

This shows God's overwhelming interest in everything about us, and the world He created. It illustrates His watchfulness, and His loving care. Then Franklin called for prayer. Why bother if God isn't paying attention, doesn't care, or is long gone?

A skeptic might say Franklin knew his audience, and he knew how to reach and manipulate them. But even if you choose to see his words as those of a deceptive, manipulative liar, it still proves the point. He knew his audience. He knew what would move them. So, they must have been a group of Christians.

Also, if he was cynically manipulating them, he knew the advantages of beginning in prayer. It would give them a better attitude, and help them see the proceedings in a larger context. It would help them fight the impulse to

---

5. KJV
6. Matthew 10:30-31 KJV

squabble over matters of personal political power or prestige. Prayer reduces the superfluous and reveals pettiness for what it is.

But I don't believe he was lying or manipulating. A man is many things over the course of a lifetime. We often make the mistake of labeling an entire life with a single quote. But, like us, historical figures were dynamic, not static. You and I don't agree with every word we ever spoke. Franklin got to change his mind, too. This quote from the Constitutional Convention tells us what he was thinking at 81 years of age, in July of 1787 — three years before his death.

Finally, did Franklin really say it? The official records indicate only that he called for daily prayer to be led by a clergyman at the beginning of each day's proceedings. The details of Franklin's speech were passed down to us primarily by James Madison's journal from the time.

There are false versions of the Franklin story floating around. But the words recounted above come directly from Madison's Journal. His first version contained only a summary. Later he inserted into the diary the words of the speech *written in Franklin's own handwriting*. In other words, Franklin himself had to have written it for Madison. That means this is how Franklin himself remembered the wording. So, at the very least, it is a close approximation.

The quote above does not represent all early American deists, but it gives some clues. Look at the respect with which he regarded the Bible. In his speech, he showed reverence for God the Father, for Jesus, for the Bible as God's revealed word, and for God's active interventions in the affairs of humanity.

That is the stuff of which America was made. God pulled out His plumb line and measured a nation. He gave it special blessings and privileges. With the blessings, He also gave it clear responsibilities.

I'm not saying that the founders were all orthodox Christians. Jefferson, Franklin, and others were not. I'm saying that a biblical worldview permeated their thinking. And that made all the difference.

Chapter 10

THE FOUNDING DOCUMENT

THE TWO BEST-KNOWN and most important founding documents are the Constitution, and the Declaration of Independence. The Constitution contains the rules by which our democracy works. The Declaration of Independence presents the big ideas upon which the Republic was built, and the ideals it endeavors to reach.

It's no accident that Abraham Lincoln began his speech at Gettysburg with King James-style English pointing, not to the Constitution, but the Declaration. "Four score and seven years ago our fathers brought forth on this continent a new nation, conceived in liberty, and dedicated to the proposition that all men are created equal."

"Four score and seven years" equals 87. He made the speech in 1863. That means he was referring, not to 1787 and the ratification of the Constitution, but to 1776 and the signing of the Declaration of Independence.

For Lincoln, this was fundamental.

Five years earlier, on a hot August afternoon in Ottawa, Illinois, he stood with his opponent for a U.S. Senate seat from Illinois — Stephen A. Douglas. It was the first of seven debates. They followed a simple, if grueling, format. In each debate, one candidate would open with an hour-long speech. The other was then given 90 minutes in which to address the statements of the first, and make his own assertions. The first speaker then came back with a 30-minute rejoinder.

In the heat, and without seats or bleachers, more than 10,000 people watched and heard the three-hour debate. The era of soundbites and 140-character limits had not yet dawned.

WE HOLD THESE TRUTHS...

In Ottawa, Douglas went first. He decided to attack one of the themes of Lincoln's position on slavery — the Declaration of Independence. Douglas said, "Mr. Lincoln... reads from the Declaration of Independence that all men were created equal, and then asks, how can you deprive a negro of that equality which God and the Declaration of Independence awards to him?"

To big laughs at Lincoln's expense, Douglas said, "I do not question Mr. Lincoln's conscientious belief that the negro was made his equal, and hence is his brother, but for my own part, I do not regard the negro as my equal, and positively deny that he is my brother or any kin to me whatever."

It was a neat bit of politicking, playing on deep prejudices. He gave the illusion of answering Lincoln's point by simply bringing it up. But his statement flatly ignored the basic question at hand — a question that was both political and theological. Not only was Douglas denying the main point of the Declaration of Independence, he was also denying Acts 17:26 from the Bible. "He has made from one blood every nation of men to dwell on all the face of the earth." In other words, in a physical sense, the Bible says we're brothers and sisters, regardless of race.

Lincoln spoke of Douglas's "covert zeal for the spread of slavery," and then said, "I hate it because of the monstrous injustice of slavery itself. I hate it because it deprives our republican example of its just influence in the world — enables the enemies of free institutions, with plausibility, to taunt us as hypocrites — causes the real friends of freedom to doubt our sincerity, and especially because it forces so many really good men amongst ourselves into an open war with the very fundamental principles of civil liberty — criticizing the Declaration of Independence, and insisting that there is no right principle of action but self-interest."

In his case against slavery, Lincoln reached for the heart of what it is to be an American and a citizen of the United States. He found that heart in the Declaration. He said to the people of Ottawa, "There is no reason in the world why the negro is not entitled to all the natural rights enumerated in the Declaration of Independence, the right to life, liberty, and the pursuit of happiness."

Until the Thirteenth Amendment, slavery was enshrined in the Constitution even though, as I said earlier, it contradicted the Bill of Rights. Lincoln saw in the Declaration a higher ideal — one that would eventually win the day. It begins with a statement of fundamental human rights based on the existence of a God to whom such things matter.

> We hold these truths to be self-evident, that all men are created equal, that they are endowed by their Creator with certain unalienable Rights, that among these are Life, Liberty and the pursuit of Happiness.

Lincoln lost the election to Douglas, but the debates turned him into a national figure. Two years later, in 1860, the Democratic Party would split in two, with Douglas as nominee of the Northern Democrats, facing Lincoln as the Republican nominee. With the Democrats split between north and south, Lincoln won the presidency with less than 40% of the popular vote.

A DREAM FROM A CREED

The night of August 27, 1963, Martin Luther King Jr. sat in the lobby of the Willard Hotel in Washington. He was still working on the speech he would give the next day at the culmination of the March on Washington. He hoped and believed it would be a pivotal day in American history. Dr. King told colleagues he wanted the speech to be "like the Gettysburg address."

He sought the advice of his team. That advice was all over the map. One of his advisors said, "Don't use the lines about 'I have a dream.' It's trite, it's cliché. You've used it too many times already."

Finally, King said, "I am now going upstairs to my room to counsel with my Lord. I will see you all tomorrow."[1]

The next day, somewhere between 250,000 and 500,000 people gathered on the Washington mall. They heard celebrities sing and speechify — some of it exhilarating, and some of it a bit boring.

Dr. King began his address in Lincolnesque manner with a tribute to Lincoln, the man on whose memorial steps he stood:

---

1. *Parting the Waters: America in the King Years 1954-63* by Taylor Branch, Simon & Schuster, 1988

Five score years ago, a great American, in whose symbolic shadow we stand today, signed the Emancipation Proclamation. This momentous decree came as a great beacon light of hope to millions of Negro slaves who had been seared in the flames of withering injustice. It came as a joyous daybreak to end the long night of their captivity. But one hundred years later, the Negro still is not free....

In a sense we've come to our nation's capital to cash a check. When the architects of our republic wrote the magnificent words of the Constitution and the Declaration of Independence, they were signing a promissory note to which every American was to fall heir. This note was a promise that all men, yes, black men as well as white men, would be guaranteed the "unalienable Rights" of "Life, Liberty and the pursuit of Happiness."

King quoted the prophet Amos. "We will not be satisfied until 'justice rolls down like waters, and righteousness like a mighty stream.'"[2]

In the "I Have a Dream" section, he quoted from Isaiah. "I have a dream that one day 'every valley shall be exalted,

2. Amos 5:24

and every hill and mountain shall be made low, the rough places will be made plain, and the crooked places will be made straight; and the glory of the Lord shall be revealed and all flesh shall see it together.'"[3]

In his monumental trilogy of books, *America in the King Years*, historian Taylor Branch wrote extensively about the speech. He tells what happened after Dr. King somehow got away from his prepared text. "There was no alternative but to preach," Branch said. "Knowing that he had wandered completely off his text, some of those behind him on the platform urged him on. Mahalia Jackson piped up as though in church. 'Tell them about the dream, Martin.'"[4]

Even King didn't know if he heard her words that day. Later, he would say that he forgot the rest of the speech, and just said what "came to me."

Harry Belafonte described Mahalia Jackson as "the single most powerful black woman in the United States." She thrilled audiences everywhere with her rich contralto voice. She was known as "the Queen of Gospel." In the 1950s and 1960s, she was a worldwide phenomenon.

---

3. As is often the case in quotations from memory this is a slightly inexact version of Isaiah 40:4-5 from the King James Version.
4. *Parting the Waters: America in the King Years 1954-63* by Taylor Branch, Simon & Schuster, 1988

When Dr. King said, it "came to me," it may have come because in the back of his mind he heard her voice saying, "Tell them about the dream, Martin."

Or maybe both were listening to a Third Voice. Either way, it marks the beginning of the part of the speech most people remember. The sequence began with these words:

> And so even though we face the difficulties of today and tomorrow, I still have a dream. It is a dream deeply rooted in the American dream.
>
> I have a dream that one day this nation will rise up and live out the true meaning of its creed: "We hold these truths to be self-evident, that all men are created equal."

Like Lincoln, King saw in those words something higher even than the Constitution. He saw them as a promissory note. He saw them as a creed, something that transcends mere political rhetoric. And, in fact, they are a religious creed because they speak of a Creator, and of our responsibilities to each other before Him.

NOT PERFECT

Let me interject something here about Dr. King's flaws. Earlier in this book when I mentioned him, I said, "Like America, Dr. King did not always live up to his ideals."

Maybe that was an understatement. We know King was a serial philanderer. His friend, colleague, and successor at the Southern Christian Leadership Conference, Ralph Abernathy, wrote in his autobiography, "We all understood and believed in the biblical prohibition against sex outside of marriage. It was just that he had a particularly difficult time with that temptation."

Abernathy expressed regret, and did not try to excuse their behavior. I don't excuse it either, but as we approach 60 years after King's death, it seems good to emphasize the man's heroic side. In the Bible, King David was both an adulterer and a murderer. We remember those huge moral failures, but we also relish the beauty of the Psalms he wrote.

I'm not saying we should disregard Dr. King's sin. But it seems to me that we should honor him in much the same way we honor other flawed men. We must never forget that George Washington and Thomas Jefferson owned slaves, but neither should we dismiss the amazing good they did for all the world.

The point of this section is that Lincoln, King, and other great Americans have always pointed back to the Declaration as the doctrine on which American freedom was built.

Chapter 11

NATIONAL CHARTER

Constitutional Attorney Michael Farris states that the Declaration is "the charter of our nation."[1] *Dictionary.com* defines a "Charter" as "a document, issued by a sovereign or state, outlining the conditions under which a corporation, colony, city, or other corporate body is organized, and defining its rights and privileges."

"The Declaration of the United States is our Charter. It is the legal document that made us a nation like all other nations of the world."[2]

In declaring their independence from England, the founders did not appeal to any earthly entity for the right to form a nation. Who would they have asked? They were severing themselves from the only nation that claimed jurisdiction over them. Their earthly "sovereign," King

---

1. "The Real Meaning of the Declaration of Independence" by Michael Farris, Concerned Women for America News, Volume 8, July 1986
2. Ibid.

George, would never grant this right. So, they appealed to a higher Power, a more sovereign Sovereign — the Supreme Judge of the universe.

The opening paragraph of the Declaration of Independence says:

> When in the course of human events, it becomes necessary for one people to dissolve the political bands which have connected them with another and to assume among the powers of the earth, the separate and equal station to which the Laws of Nature and Nature's God entitle them a decent respect to the opinions of mankind requires that they should declare the causes which impel them to the separation.

This did more than mention God. It said the entire Declaration was written to show all mankind why the "the Laws of Nature and Nature's God" entitled them to their own nation. They based their case on the fairness and sovereignty of God. They admitted to breaking man's law, and then appealed to a higher law — God's law.

The second paragraph of our nation's charter gives the foundation for the case that there should be a free American nation. The case rests on a theological decree.

We hold these truths to be self-evident, that all men are created equal, that they are endowed by their Creator with certain unalienable Rights, that among these are Life, Liberty and the pursuit of Happiness.

"CREATED EQUAL"

The concept of "Creator" is the lynchpin that holds the Declaration together. The logic simply does not work without God. In what meaningful way could we be equal if there is not a Creator?

In the material world of nature and human society, we are not equal. At birth, you may have better genetics, more committed parents, financial stability, better health, a cleaner environment, better aptitude for learning or sports, or be born into a nation with greater opportunity than another.

We can only be equal in our fundamental worth. That kind of worth cannot come from nature or society, but only from God. If we hold to God's system of values, then the murderer of a learning-disabled child is investigated and prosecuted in the same way as one who steals the life of a brilliant scientist. The two victims are not equal in value to society, but are equal in worth before God.

To the world, we have different values based on what we can produce. But to God, we have intrinsic value because He made us in His image.[3]

I previously pointed to Acts 17:26. "He has made from one blood every nation of men to dwell on all the face of the earth."

Romans 3:23 says, "All have sinned." That puts us all — rich or poor, influential or seemingly inconsequential — in the same mess, and with the same solution available equally to all.

Revelation 3:20 says, "Behold, I stand at the door and knock. If anyone hears My voice and opens the door, I will come in to him and dine with him, and he with Me."

The King of kings and Lord of lords offers His fellowship to "anyone." That act demonstrates the worth of everyone.

In John 3:7, Jesus said, "You must be born again." That makes us all equally needy, but with equal potential. It applies to people in all parts of the world, to all levels of wealth, all races, and both sexes. Our creation in His image, our commonality as sinners, and His universal offer of redemption are the ultimate human equalizers.

---

3. Genesis 1:27

Acts 10:34 says it all. "God shows no partiality."

John 3:16 says, "For God so loved the world that He gave His only begotten Son, that whoever believes in Him should not perish but have everlasting life."

"Whoever" … "anyone" … "the world" … "no partiality." These were the words and phrases that inspired a special nation to know that we were created by a real and personal God.

ULTIMATE VALUE BESTOWED ON ALL

If you're going to sell a car or a house, the value is… whatever someone is willing to pay. You can list any price you want, but unless a buyer agrees to pay it, that price is just a number. If I decide to sell my computer, I might put a price on it of a million dollars. Is it worth that much? Only if I can find someone willing and able to pay that much.

God pronounced human worth when He paid the price for human redemption. 1 Corinthians 6:20 says, "You have been bought with a price."[4]

The price paid establishes worth. What was the price God paid? Titus 2:14 says, "Our great God and Savior Jesus Christ… gave Himself for us, that He might redeem us from every lawless deed."

4. NASB

1 Corinthians 15:3 puts it simply and succinctly. "Christ died for our sins."

The life of Jesus poured out on the cross represents a value we can only begin to fathom.

Yet it is not an occasion for pride. The value He chooses to assign to human beings is not based on anything we have done. It's simply a gift. We have been "endowed by" our Creator. To be "endowed" is not the same as to "earn." We are not valuable based on something we deserved, but on something God chose to do.

Romans 5:6-8 puts it like this. "When we were still without strength, in due time Christ died for the ungodly. For scarcely for a righteous man will one die; yet perhaps for a good man someone would even dare to die. But God demonstrates His own love toward us, in that while we were still sinners, Christ died for us."

By His own sovereign choice, and not because of anything we have done, He has pronounced every human being valuable beyond human understanding or ability to express. God endowed human beings with worth. That worth does not come from government, money, academia, nor any institution of man. It is the gift of God. Therefore, no institution of man can take it away.

EXISTENCE BASED IN THE RECOGNITION OF GOD

Those who try to eliminate every vestige of Christianity from American life need to recognize that the nation's founding idea is a theological one. It is a creed that sprang from the teachings of Jesus Christ.

Our primary founding document says that God's law supersedes man's law, and sets itself to operate on His higher plane of law. By appealing to God's law, the founding fathers made a commitment to that law. The "charter of our nation" stands on the reality of God, His inherent fairness, and a commitment to His ways.

Remember what I said earlier. America's founders could not appeal to their earthly sovereign in declaring independence, so they appealed to a more Sovereign sovereign. Following human law, there would be no United States of America. It exists because they appealed to something infinitely higher — God's law.

AMERICAN PLUMB LINE

Michael Farris went on to say that, as the charter, the Declaration of Independence "doesn't tell us how we are going to run our country — that is what our Constitution does. In a corporation, the Charter is higher than the

By-laws and the By-laws must be interpreted to be in agreement with the Charter. Therefore, the Constitution of the United States must be in agreement with the Declaration of the United States (more commonly known as the Declaration of Independence)."[5]

Even as we judge all our laws by the Constitution, we must read the Constitution by the light emanating from the Declaration of Independence. That was the approach of Abraham Lincoln in arguing against slavery, and that of Martin Luther King in arguing for civil rights.

Farris said, "The most important statement in our Declaration is that we want to operate under the laws of God."[6]

That is why the idea of a plumb line is such a big deal to America. The Declaration, the thing that set the United States apart as its own national entity among the nations, says that we are a nation under God's laws. Therefore, all the other laws of our country should be consistent with the law of God. If not, we violate the charter.

The founding documents are America's plumb line. We began like Israel, proclaiming God's law supreme. And now we are watching America violate her charter — cut

---

5. "The Real Meaning of the Declaration of Independence" by Michael Farris, Concerned Women for America News, Volume 8, July 1986
6. ibid.

herself off from the root system that grants her life and fruitfulness.

God said to Israel, "You are out of plumb. You are crooked. Judgment is here!" He is saying the same thing now to the United States of America.

OUT OF PLUMB

Americans can amend the Constitution, but the Declaration of Independence simply exists — unamendable and out of the reach of the fashions of political correctness.

Will a federal judge someday rule the Declaration "unconstitutional," and forbid its "doctrine" from being read in American classrooms? At Christmas, cities get sued if they have a manger scene. Judges across the land are ordering the removal of monuments to the Ten Commandments. Yet the Declaration of Independence is as "religious" as any of these.

Americans work every day to remove all reminders — not only of God and His law, but also of His mercy and grace. We don't just remove the Ten Commandments, but the cross. Crosses on public-owned lands are being torn down. Cities are removing it from their logos and coats of arms. Secularists want to burn the bridge between God and man; and between America and her heritage.

Cities and other institutions generally follow the path of least resistance. Giving in is easier than fighting back. They get rid of the cross because it might offend someone. They forget the offense of spiritual sterility and nothingness.

Judges and politicians play a kind of tether ball with the cross of the Lord Jesus. They tell us we must remove it to insure the dignity and freedom of the individual. But as they cut down those crosses, they're cutting away America's roots. From such roots flow the very freedom and dignity the root-cutters say they want to preserve.

Instead of operating according to the laws of God as the nation promised, America today is trying to remove every trace of every memory of Him.

Revisionist historians try to tell us that America never really revered God or His word. But here's the deal. Remember the crosses and monuments to the Ten Commandments the humanists are constantly working to remove? Someone put them there. Someone started traditions of prayer in school, and at the opening of Congress.

The God-things now painted as offensive, were once the roots that nourished and anchored our republic.

Chapter 12

FOUNDING INSTITUTIONS

GOD ORDAINED CERTAIN INSTITUTIONS for the preservation of the human race. We see them in all societies, but they vary a great deal in their effectiveness. The health of these institutions is a barometer of the overall health of the society within which they exist.

The thing often referred to as "American exceptionalism" came into being because in the United States, these institutions were built to a large degree on biblical principles. Until recent decades, their connection to Bible truth gave them health and strength.

MARRIAGE

Marriage is not and has never been a one-person show. It takes two. Any time I talk about divorce, I am aware that some of those reading these words have been through divorce. In many cases, I'm talking to the wronged party in the divorce.

Ironically, the one most victimized is often the one who feels the most guilt. The one with the tender heart, who tried like crazy to make things work against all odds, tends to beat himself or herself up the most when the marriage ends. It doesn't always work that way, but it does more times than not.

I want to talk about divorce, but I don't want to slam you over the head if you've been through one. If you right-fully carry guilt after a divorce, you should confess and repent — just as with other areas of your life. If you've already done that, then trust God to keep His word.

This section is not here to make you feel guilty or blue. I'm not talking about you personally, but about overall trends in American society.

The family stands as the most important single institution for the preservation of humanity. And at the heart of family, we find marriage. The health of marriage as a national institution is a key factor in the moral, psychological, economic, and academic health of the nation.

Data from the Center for Disease Control and Prevention (CDC) say there were 3 divorces for every 100 marriages in the 1860s. That number would rise to 26 out of a 100 in the 1960s, 48 in the 1970s, and more than 50 in the 1980s. About half the children born in the 1970s saw their parents divorce. From 1974 forward, more than a million kids a year lived in a home where the parents divorced. Half of those children were age 6 or below.

Studies show numerous benefits to staying married. Want to live longer? Stay married. Want financial security? Stay married. Want a sense of security and belonging? Stay married. And, despite what Hollywood teaches, the best sex-life is a monogamous one with your wife or husband.

Judith Wallerstein's landmark book, *The Unexpected Legacy of Divorce* came as the result of a 25-year study of divorce and the children of divorce. It found that children usually cope well with divorce during childhood. Her team found that the most difficult side-effects take place when the kids become adults. In significantly higher numbers than adults from intact homes, they have more difficulty with commitment, go to extremes to avoid conflict, and tend to feel that their own relationships are doomed.

In reviewing Wallerstein's book for the *New York Times*, Margaret Talbot wrote, "If you grew up in the 1970's, then you remember a time when the very phrase 'staying together for the sake of the children' sounded hopelessly Victorian. Unhappily married couples, so the thinking went, were doing their children a favor by divorcing.... Divorce was a crisis from which children would quickly bounce back. For years, this notion hung on more or less unassailed in dinner-party wisdom, psychology textbooks and sitcoms. Only in the last decade or so has it begun to seem more self-serving than truthful."[1]

This is a big picture of divorce. It works differently for different people. Don't let this make you feel like your choices, or your children's choices, are foreordained.

Nevertheless, when we look at these tendencies multiplied by a million divorces a year, the size of the tragedy begins to strike home. On average, a divorce occurs in the United States every 36 seconds. And every one of them hurts. America is staggering under this multiplied pain.

THE FAMILY

The United States won World War II and survived the Great Depression because young men and women stood heroically in the face of adversity. Most of them came from intact families where even non-Christian mothers and fathers instilled in them principles from the Bible. Their moral grit strengthened and buoyed them in the face of calamity.

---

1. *The Price of Divorce* by Margaret Talbot, the New York Times, October 1, 2000

What would happen now if America faced similar tests? Gold stars and "attaboys" don't put steel in anyone's resolve. Godliness does. Family stability does.

The Brookings Institution reports, "Since 1970, out-of-wedlock birth rates have soared. In 1965, 24 percent of black infants and 3.1 percent of white infants were born to single mothers. By 1990 the rates had risen to 64 percent for black infants, 18 percent for whites. Every year about one million more children are born into fatherless families. If we have learned any policy lesson well over the past 25 years, it is that for children living in single-parent homes, the odds of living in poverty are great. The policy implications of the increase in out-of-wedlock births are staggering."[2]

The CDC data shows that 41% of all 2012 births were out-of-wedlock. Among African-Americans, that number was 72%. It is the single biggest indicator of poverty. Intact black families make more money, their children do far better in school, and are much less likely to get into trouble with the law.

Out-of-wedlock births hit a peak in the late 2000s and leveled off. But the damage continues at approximately the same awful pace. The pain and suffering are incalculable. These are not just statistics, but human beings.

---

2. "An Analysis of Out-Of-Wedlock Births in the United States" by George A. Akerlof and Janet L. Yellen, August 1, 1996

EDUCATION

Children go from the home to the school, and, despite the heroic work of so many American teachers, things go from bad to worse.

In America's early days, the Bible served as an important textbook in schools. Even before the Declaration of Independence, there was *The New England Primer*. By 1737, its use had spread throughout the colonies. It was more than a primer on reading. It was a handbook on life — full of the Bible and specifically Christian doctrine.

In teaching the alphabet, the Primer said "A" was for Adam. "In Adam's fall, We sinned all." "B" was for Bible. "Heaven to find; The Bible Mind." "C" was for Christ, "Christ crucify'd, For sinners dy'd." This kind of teaching took the child all the way through the alphabet to "Z." "Zacchaeus he, Did climb the Tree, Our Lord to see."

It contained "An Alphabet of Lessons for Youth" which began like this:

A wise son maketh a glad father, but a foolish son is the heaviness of his mother.

*B*etter is a little with the fear of the Lord, than great treasure & trouble therewith.

*C*ome unto Christ all ye that labor and are heavy laden and He will give you rest.

*D*o not the abominable thing which I hate saith the Lord.

*E*xcept a man be born again, he cannot see the kingdom of God.

Printer Benjamin Harris published the first version of *The New England Primer* in 1687. That means it predates the founding of the country by almost a hundred years. Until 1790, it was the primary textbook in American schools. Soldiers who would fight America's revolution grew up on the lessons of this book. It was heavily used throughout the country for more than 200 years.

Imagine a kid coming home from public school today, and talking about the amazing lesson he or she just learned. "Except a man be born again, he cannot see the kingdom of God."

Get the lawyers ready because someone's child felt "uncomfortable" at school today. Call the police, and let them know there's been a hate crime! In those days, the Bible was an expected part of life. Now, the powers-that-be try to wrap the Bible in layers of lies, then hide it away from public schools and public forums.

I'm not saying we have a culture in crisis because we no longer use *The New England Primer*. I am saying that the greatest danger facing the U.S. is its severe moral decline. That decline directly corresponds with the level of esteem in which our country holds the Bible. Education illustrates that point better than anything else.

America lost her moorings when she cut herself off from God's revealed word. Individual Americans have always had all kinds of different ideas about the Bible. But they swore on it in court, or when coming into office. They did that because the population almost universally held it in the highest esteem.

HIGHER EDUCATION

Harvard University, that bastion of secular humanism, atheism, and elitism, was established to train missionaries. Its motto was *veritas christo et ecclesiae*. That means "Truth for Christ and the Church."

In the Spring of 2016, angry Harvard students tried to shout down African-American pro-life activist Ryan Bomberger. They called him a "racist," and said he hates black people. Bomberger said, "Most of the time I couldn't respond to everything going on. Students cursed and yelled at me repeatedly, especially an LGBT activist."

Why were they so outraged? Because he correctly pointed out Planned Parenthood's inherent racism. The organization was founded by Margaret Sanger. She was a racist who worried that the people she called "the lower classes" were producing too many babies. Even today, Planned Parenthood concentrates its clinics in minority neighborhoods. As a result, in New York City, more black babies are aborted than are born alive.

It outraged the Harvard elites that anyone dare tell them something so awful — even though it was true. They snapped. Instead of reasonably discussing the issues, they went berserk.

Much of the radicalism of the 1960s was born in what became known as the Free Speech Movement on the campus of UC Berkeley. But the grandchildren of those 60s radicals have come to oppose free speech.

In an editorial for the *Los Angeles Times*, Professors Howard Gillman and Erwin Chemerinsky told about teaching a freshman seminar on freedom of speech on various college campuses. "From the beginning of our course," they wrote, "we were surprised by the often unanimous willingness of our students to support efforts to restrict and punish a wide range of expression."

A survey at Yale showed that 72% of students support a university taking disciplinary action against "any student or faculty member on campus who uses language that is considered racist, sexist, homophobic or otherwise offensive."

The Bill of Rights' guarantee of free speech not only guarantees speech, but something else as well. It guarantees that we will all be offended. We will hear things we don't like or with which we disagree. But a high percentage of the young people populating college campuses believe that if they don't like what you say, then you don't have a right to say it. Instead of reason and discussion, they are all about silencing and censorship.

In the summer of 2016, Princeton University released a four-page memo called, "Guidelines for Using Gender Inclusive Language." They wrote, "Gender-inclusive language is writing and speaking about people in a manner that does not use gender-based words."

Perhaps unknowingly, they just stripped the English language of some of its richest and most powerful words. "Husband, wife, man, and woman," to name a few, help us understand one another. They cross cultural barriers, while their weak, gender-inclusive stand-ins raise cultural barriers. The stand-ins are imprecise, and lack history and human texture.

One of the most dramatic and striking television show openings ever created was for the 1960s series, *Ben Casey*. The great actor Sam Jaffe played Ben Casey's mentor, Dr. Zorba.

The episodes began with a hand drawing symbols on a blackboard. Each symbol represented a word spoken by Dr. Zorba. *"Man... woman... birth... death... infinity."*

Those are five of the most dramatic expressions in any language. *"Man... woman."* What an awesome story those words tell. "So God created man in His own image; in the image of God He created him; male and female He created them."[3]

The science fiction adventure, *Logan's Run*, describes a world of emptiness and sterility where life centers on a meaningless pursuit of pleasure. In the story, the two protagonists escape the terrible cleanness of their domed city. They find the remains of an ancient Washington, DC. In a cemetery, they see grave markers with the words, "Beloved Husband," and "Beloved Wife." Later, in the meaning of those words, they find their humanity.[4,5]

---

3. Genesis 1:27
4. *Logan's Run*, Metro-Goldwyn-Mayer, directed by Michael Anderson, screenplay by David Zelag Goodman based on the novel, Logan's Run by William F. Nolan, 1976.
5. Warning: Despite its PG rating, *Logan's Run* contains a surprising level of nudity. The first use of the PG-13 rating didn't begin until 8 years later.

Princeton's bow to political correctness is typical of universities across America. It eliminates some of the richest, most evocative words in the English language — man, woman, husband, wife, boy, girl, male, female.

The fact that I followed the old tradition and placed those words with male before female will offend some. If I put the feminine first, it would offend others. But most stunning of all, is that in our present warped society, basic words like wife and husband, regardless of order or context, can be offensive. We're to say "partners" — even if we're talking about traditional heterosexual marriage.

We are losing something precious, and I mean really precious. We're losing ourselves.

In this stripping away of human essence, universities lead the way. In too many areas to recount here, the educational establishment is robbing Americans of the truth and richness of human existence, and replacing it with frail, sleazy substitutes. You will not learn the real joys of sex at your local university's "Sex Week." You'll learn it in the moral security of biblical precepts.

LAW AND GOVERNMENT

In 2013, the State of Colorado voted to legalize marijuana for recreational use starting in 2014. Other states have followed, but Colorado was first, and that action makes a good demarcation point for the moment when the old cultural principles became fringe, and what was formerly the counterculture went mainstream. The states that make marijuana legal do so even though the sale, possession, and use of marijuana remain a federal crime. The God-ordained institution of human law is breaking down at the point of feelings.

Marijuana was not mainstreamed because of science. The data showing adverse effects from marijuana use are far stronger now than they were, for instance, in the 1960s. That's partly because today's marijuana contains a far higher percentage of THC, marijuana's psychoactive ingredient. It's stronger and more harmful.

The choice to legalize weed is not about data, or thoughtful reasoning. It's about desire. People want to get high — facts or no facts; federal law or no federal law.

Courts are supposed to interpret law as written by appropriate legislatures, and to judge the constitutionality of those laws. But in recent years, courts have insinuated themselves into the role of legislators. They interpret and judge laws as a means to push their own political agendas. That's fine for elected members of the legislature, but never for judges.

The courts are undermining the Constitution that empowers them. That's like sawing off the limb you're sitting on.

It's the same thing for an overreaching President. It is not the President's job to create law. Again, that's the job of Congress. The President leads the Executive Branch of government. He or she is the nation's chief executive. That word comes from the root word, "execute." Congress creates law and the President executes, or implements, the law.

An overreaching President is like an activist judge — undermining the constitutional source of his own power.

Later, we'll look at the phenomenon of "lawlessness" in more depth. Here it is enough to say that, like marriage, the family, and education, the institution of law and government has turned from God-inspired integrity to whimsical, feelings-based standards that bend with the winds of moral fashion.

Chapter 13

PRELUDE TO JUDGMENT

ANCIENT ISRAEL REJECTED GOD... while remaining highly religious. Their priests, pastors, and prophets gave the people exactly what they wanted — the green light to go to a temple, and after leaving, sin freely. Israel's religious leaders made the word of God of no effect.[1]

But it wasn't just the religious leaders. Their politicians were also corrupt. The judges were corrupt. The kings were corrupt. They rewrote God's law. They interpreted or reinterpreted the laws for their own benefit and the benefit of the elite class. They wrote God out of their lives — all while remaining extremely religious.

Under God's rules, Israel was to hold sacrificial worship at only one place — the Temple in Jerusalem. But by the time of Amos, the people of the northern kingdom had long since abandoned the single Temple of God and

1. Mark 7:6-13

traded it in for a multitude of temples. They had more religion than ever... but they didn't know God.

AMERICA FALLS, PERSON BY PERSON

2 Timothy 3:5 speaks of people "having a form of godliness but denying its power." That means people with spirituality — perhaps a religion or religiosity, perhaps a highly-developed sense of superstition — but without the God through Whom life flows, and without reverence for His word.

Today we often hear, "I'm a very spiritual person." Israel was full of spiritual people... even as it fell under God's judgment. They were spiritual, but they rejected the things God told them. In so doing, they denied the power of God.

As it happened in ancient Israel, so it is happening today. In crucial ways, America today mirrors Israel just before God's judgment fell. They were religious, yet without God. In those days, God said through Amos that judgment would come to Judah because they "despised the law of the Lord, and have not kept His commandments."[2]

That's them then, and it's us now!

We live in the middle of a cultural crisis. Our discourse is mean-spirited. We live in a climate of fear. We treat rights

2. Amos 2:4 NIV

and values as fashions — disposable, and easily replaced with a constant supply line of ever-changing new models based on the latest fads.

People on the political right and left, believers and atheists, all lament the loss of our moorings. It feels like we're adrift because we are. We are without an anchor even as a series of storms loom on the horizon.

CHILD SACRIFICE

Earlier, I said, "God will judge America for treating children as disposable." Let's revisit that idea in light of what happened to Israel shortly before it fell under God's severe judgment. It's not possible to fully grasp America's precarious position without understanding what a big deal child sacrifice is in the Bible.

God repeatedly warned the Children of Israel about the dangers of conforming their ways to those of their wicked neighbors. Deuteronomy 12:29-30 says, "When the Lord your God cuts off from before you the nations which you go to dispossess, and you displace them and dwell in their land, take heed to yourself that you are not ensnared to follow them, after they are destroyed from before you, and that you do not inquire after their gods, saying, 'How did these nations serve their gods? I also will do likewise.'"

Victory on the battlefield, or in an election, is lost if we then conform to the values of those we defeated.

The next verse, Deuteronomy 12:31, says, "You shall not worship the Lord your God in that way; for every abomination to the Lord which He hates they have done to their gods; for they burn even their sons and daughters in the fire to their gods."

That's talking about burning children to death as a sacrifice to idols. In Leviticus 18:21, God said, "You shall not let any of your descendants pass through the fire to Molech."

Psalm 106:37-38 says of Israel, "They even sacrificed their sons And their daughters to demons, And shed innocent blood, The blood of their sons and daughters, Whom they sacrificed to the idols of Canaan; And the land was polluted with blood."

We live in an age that is rightfully concerned about pollution of the environment. But when God looks at a nation, He sees the blood of babies as the ultimate contamination.

Jeremiah 32:35 says, "And they built the high places of Baal which are in the Valley of the Son of Hinnom, to cause their sons and their daughters to pass through the fire to Molech, which I did not command them, nor did it come into My mind that they should do this abomination, to cause Judah to sin."

Hinnom is outside the old city of Jerusalem to the west and south. It connects to the Kidron Valley, which lies between the Temple Mount and the Mount of Olives, east of the old city.

The medieval French Rabbi Rashi put in writing the traditional Jewish understanding of how this worked. Molech (sometimes spelled "Moloch") "was made of brass; and they heated him from his lower parts; and his hands being stretched out, and made hot, they put the child between his hands, and it was burnt; when it vehemently cried out; but the priests beat a drum, that the father might not hear the voice of his son, and his heart might not be moved."

Today, a different drumbeat sounds, but it serves the same purpose. It is the sound of politicians crying out for "a woman's right to choose." What a choice! It's the sound of the media pretending that humans in the womb are not human at all. It's the sound of cash registers ringing, and of high fashion lifestyles built on the deaths of children. The drums say, "Nothing to see here folks. A woman can do what she wants with her own body. Move along."

But the body in question is not the woman's. The body I'm talking about has its own DNA, separate from the woman. The mother is always a female, but the body in question can be either male or female — because it's a different body. It has its own heart, brain, and soul.

When you visit Israel these days, you can drive past the Valley of Hinnom, also known as Gehenna, a word that came to mean hell. Because of the child sacrifice there, the Valley of Hinnom came to be viewed as cursed. Today, as you drive by it on a modern road, it's hard to fathom what once went on in that valley.

HUMAN SACRIFICE IN AMERICA

The Smithsonian Institute talks about human sacrifice in America. "Wisconsin's Aztalan State Park is home to a mysterious pyramidal mound built by the prehistoric Native Americans who once lived there. Excavations of the site have yielded intriguing, and grisly, findings."[3]

Wisconsin? Really? It seems far removed from the 21st century. But it's not. The silent screams of the fifty-nine million babies that have been aborted in the United States since Roe v. Wade in 1973 tell us emphatically that it is not far away at all.

To encourage any form of infanticide puts a society on precarious ground. God calls such activity an "abomination." Child sacrifice is the main reason He finally brought the hammer down on Judah. In Matthew 18:10, Jesus said, "Take heed that you do not despise one of these little ones, for I say to you that in heaven their angels always see the face of My Father who is in heaven."

---

3. Smithsonianmag.com, "In Wisconsin, Evidence of Human Sacrifice."

REWIRED FOR EVIL

"And Judah did evil in the sight of the Lord," according to 1 Kings, "and they provoked him to jealousy with their sins which they had committed, above all that their fathers had done. For they also built them high places, and images, and groves, on every high hill, and under every green tree. And there were also sodomites in the land: and they did according to all the abominations of the nations which the Lord cast out before the children of Israel."[4]

Ancient Israel's national evils of infanticide, idolatry, and homosexuality have become the national evils of America today.

For saying that, I am labeled "a hater." So be it. I will not allow the blood of someone else's life to be on my hands. Call me "a hater" if you want, but "God is love."[5] That means He cannot be a hater, and His word cannot be hateful.

As in Israel before judgment fell, we have judges, politicians, and religious leaders rewriting the nation's laws, and reinterpreting God's law. We have fallen a long way from the beginning of our country — just as Israel had. They killed the Prophets — even sawing them in two.[6]

---

4. 1 Kings 14:22-24 KJV
5. 1 John 4:8, 15
6. Hebrews 11:37

Why? Because they said what some of God's servants are still saying today — that sin is sin.

Patrick Wyett, writing for RaptureReady.com, asked, "Can a nation turn from evil?"[7] Then he quoted from 1 Kings 15, "And Asa did that which was right in the eyes of the Lord, as did David his father. And he took away the sodomites out of the land, and removed all the idols that his fathers had made."[8]

Asa repented, but the next generation went right back to the old evil ways. A spring works by constantly pushing itself into its old shape. That's how Israel was.

Wyett goes on to say, "As Judah demonstrates, there exists an opportunity to turn from sin. However, when a city, nation or even the entire world becomes so wicked that sin becomes inseparable from its culture, indeed it becomes the culture, then God's judgment is inevitable."

A SUDDEN CONCERN

Many years ago, a reporter from NBC News telephoned Tim LaHaye. They were preparing a prime-time special on "teaching values." The reporter asked LaHaye,

---

7. "Living Under Judgment, Part II" by Patrick Wyett, RaptureReady.com, not dated
8. 1 Kings 15:11-12 KJV

"How can we return to teaching values without violating the first amendment?"[9]

He was really asking how to teach values without teaching about or acknowledging God. Of course, that's an incorrect interpretation of the First Amendment. As LaHaye pointed out, if a church is on fire, the government-owned Fire Department comes to put it out. The First Amendment says, "Congress shall make no law respecting an establishment of religion, or prohibiting the free exercise thereof." It says nothing about a wall of separation.

But the question made LaHaye curious. He asked the reporter, "Why this sudden concern?"

The newsman replied that he had talked to federal Department of Education officials, both local and national politicians, and to many parents. He gave a litany of things happening in society that are symptoms of a nation in severe moral decline.

LaHaye later wrote, "He was simply affirming the biblical maxim that we reap what we sow. As a nation, we are reaping 50 years of secularist teachings on morals in our schools — and we don't like it."[10]

9. *Faith of Our Founding Fathers* by Tim LaHaye, Wolgemuth & Hyatt Publishers, 1987
10. ibid.

The reporter wanted to know how we can have the good life and be happy with good families, but keep God out of it. People have wanted to know that for thousands of years. The answer is that the good life with good families and children reared to have strong moral character can last only a short time without God.

In America today, we are beginning to reap what we have sown, and it's not pretty. None of it would be a surprise to our Founding Fathers. They knew that the thing they were creating would not work without God.

When a people sow seeds of open rebellion against God, they reap that rebellion in their own children.

CONSIDER YOUR WAYS

It doesn't stop there. Turning from the true God to the gods of comfort and pleasure affects every aspect of a society.

Through the prophet Haggai, the Lord said, "'Is it time for you yourselves to dwell in your paneled houses, and this temple to lie in ruins?' Now therefore, thus says the Lord of hosts: 'Consider your ways! You have sown much, and bring in little; You eat, but do not have enough; You drink, but you are not filled with drink; You clothe yourselves, but no one is warm; And he who earns wages, Earns wages to put into a bag with holes.'"[11]

We all feel at times that our money is going into a bag with holes. If you want to see an extreme example, take a look at the budget of the United States. We spend more on defense than all the other nations of the world *combined*, even as we watch our military power decay before our eyes.

We throw more money at education than any generation in our history. Even so, vast numbers of our kids grow up without even a rudimentary ability to read, write, or do math. We have communications tools that previous generations could not have imagined, but we can't teach our children basic values. We earn money only to put it in a bag with holes.

God's answer? "Consider your ways!"[12] As a nation, America must consider her ways. Are they the ways of righteousness and peace? Are they the ways of God? No!

Through Haggai, the Lord continued to speak. "'Consider your ways! Go up to the mountains and bring wood and build the temple, that I may take pleasure in it and be glorified,' says the Lord. 'You looked for much, but

---

11. Haggai 1:4-6
12. Haggai 1:7

indeed it came to little; and when you brought it home, I blew it away. Why?' says the Lord of hosts. 'Because of My house that is in ruins, while every one of you runs to his own house. Therefore the heavens above you withhold the dew, and the earth withholds its fruit.'"[13]

In other words, famine is coming! The spigot of heaven is being turned off. The heavens "withhold the dew, and the earth withholds its fruit."

We're getting a strong taste of this in the U.S. even as I write these words.

"For I called for a drought on the land and the mountains, on the grain and the new wine and the oil, on whatever the ground brings forth, on men and livestock, and on all the labor of your hands."[14]

Remember the word of the Lord. "Consider your ways."

THE COMING JUDGMENT

God's most severe judgment against sin took place in the Garden of Eden. When Adam and Eve sinned, they died spiritually, and the pain of death was loosed on the whole world and all the generations that have followed them.

---

13. Haggai 1:7-10
14. Haggai 1:11

The second most severe judgment took place in the days of Noah. "Then the Lord saw that the wickedness of man was great in the earth, and that every intent of the thoughts of his heart was only evil continually."[15]

Romans 1:21 applies to the world in Noah's day, and to America in our day. "Although they knew God, they did not glorify Him as God, nor were thankful, but became futile in their thoughts, and their foolish hearts were darkened." The King James Version says, they "became vain in their imaginations."

One of America's leading exports is entertainment. But we're not just exporting fun. We're exporting values. Romans 1:21 perfectly describes most of the content in games, films, music, television, and the rest. They come from vain imaginations and foolish hearts that are growing ever darker with depraved violence, sexual promiscuity, and bizarre combinations of the two.

We see thousands of advertisements a day. Madison Avenue designed most of them to excite in our hearts "the lust of the flesh, the lust of the eyes, and the pride of life."[16] To sell their products, marketing professionals have become exceedingly proficient at amplifying evil thoughts and imagination.

---

15. Genesis 6:5
16. 1 John 2:16

Jesus said, "As the days of Noah were, so also will the coming of the Son of Man be."[17]

We now live in those times.

17. Matthew 24:37

Chapter 14

PROGRESSIVELY PERILOUS TIMES

In 2 Timothy 3:1, Paul writes, "But know this, that in the last days perilous times will come."

For Americans, the last half of the twentieth century became a golden age of safety. Nuclear catastrophe loomed, but didn't happen. On the other hand, lots of good things did happen. In 1930, life expectancy for an American was 59.7 years. By the end of the century, it had risen 30%. We had the best medicine, the best food supply, the best housing, the best police and fire departments, and the best military in the history of the world.

That's mostly still true. But if you ask the average American if he or she feels safer today than 20 years ago, most will admit to an increasing level of anxiety. Even those who only occasionally read or watch news reports, sense that we live in progressively perilous times. They're right.

Nuclear weapons prove the point. Many thought the nuclear threat had ended with the collapse of the Soviet Union in the early 1990s. Today, these unthinkable weapons are falling into the hands of the most dangerous people on earth; people who live for the day when they can harm or destroy the United States.

This points to another problem. Weapons of mass destruction will not go away or get into fewer hands. They will get into more. As bad as things are, they will get worse. And WMDs are the tip of the iceberg.

The Greek word translated "perilous" means, "hard to take, hard to bear, troublesome, fierce, very dangerous, savage, and strength is reduced." So, according to the Bible, the coming days won't just be "hard to bear," but "savage" and "fierce." The perils of perilous times will increase exponentially as the world gets closer to the end of the age.

THE DANGER WITHIN

The verses that go on to describe "perilous times" don't directly mention war, an economic collapse, or natural disasters. Every descriptor of "perilous times" in these verses relates to the deterioration of the morals and character of the people populating those times. In other words, *we are the problem.*

Look at the end of verse 1 and the beginning of verse 2 together. "...perilous times will come: For men will be..." and then it lists some of the striking characteristics of end times humanity. The key word is "For" at the beginning of verse 2. It joins the passage together. It's saying, times will be perilous and here's why.

"For men will be lovers of themselves, lovers of money, boasters, proud, blasphemers, disobedient to parents, unthankful, unholy, unloving, unforgiving, slanderers, without self-control, brutal, despisers of good, traitors, headstrong, haughty, lovers of pleasure rather than lovers of God, having a form of godliness but denying its power. And from such people turn away!"[1]

We know that all these things have characterized much of humanity throughout history. So why did the Holy Spirit inspire Paul to write these words specifically about the last days? Because in the time just before Christ's return, pride, blasphemy, brutality, and the rest will be ratcheted up to an unprecedented level. If it will be business as usual, why mention it?

LOVERS OF SELF

Compare the words in 2 Timothy 3 to America today. "Men will be lovers of themselves." You might say, they

---

1. 2 Timothy 3:2-5

will be full of themselves. Does that sound like American political and business leaders, successful musicians, athletes, and other entertainers? At every turn, we see conspicuous consumption, self-reverence, and self-importance.

During what's known as "awards season" in Hollywood each year, the film industry falls all over itself trying to congratulate itself. Each actor describes the TV program he's on, or the movie he was in as "groundbreaking." They use their acceptance speeches to try to straighten out all those poor people in "flyover country." Not every actor, but the ones looking down on us from the heights of their own perceived self-importance are, classically, "lovers of self."

Our educational philosophies and advertising methodologies teach even ordinary folk the deification of self. We have *People Magazine*. We have *Us Magazine* which is about... us. Then there's *Self Magazine*. I wonder what that's about. We have Facebook where we tell everyone all about ourselves, and check our daily count of friends and "likes."

A few years ago, Microsoft wanted to make sure everyone remembered whose computer they were using, and whose music they were listening to, so they labeled things, "My Computer," "My Music," "My Videos." Commercials are full of the phrase, "You deserve it!" They want you to buy the car you deserve, go to the places you deserve, eat the foods you deserve. Why do you deserve it? Who knows? Apparently, you just do... if you have the money, or credit.

Now we have the selfie. What a fantastic word to describe "lovers of themselves." "Selfie" was one of the words of the year for 2013. Let me be clear that being on Facebook is not evil, and taking a selfie is not a sin. But look what the obsession with these things tells us about our society.

I read an account of a young woman standing in an airport for over an hour, camera in hand, working on different poses and facial expressions. Pursuit of the perfect selfie consumes the days of many Americans. Of course, the young woman in the airport may have had a completely altruistic motive. Maybe she wanted to encourage a husband serving in the military far from home. On the other hand, she may have just wanted her friends to think she was "hot."

In the last few years, selfies killed more people than sharks.[2] We live in a self-centered generation. People are "lovers of themselves."

In February of 2017, the Society for Personality and Social Psychology released a study that found that millennials are perceived as the most narcissistic generation...

2. "More people have died from selfies than shark attacks this year" by Cailey Rizzo, *Mashable*, 9-21-2015

even among millennials. The study says they hate the label, but agree with it.

In May of 2016, a U.S. Congressman wrote an anonymous tell-all book about his job. He wrote, "My main job is to keep my job, to get reelected. It takes precedence over everything…. We spend money we don't have and blithely mortgage the future with a wink and a nod. Screw the next generation."

If that were just one Congressman's assessment, we could brush it off. But even a casual follower of the workings on Capitol Hill knows that it's almost universally true. To members of Congress, job-one is winning the next election. Forget the next generation. I want more for me now!

LOVERS OF MONEY

Men will be "lovers of money."[3]

That verse goes along with 1 Timothy 6:10. "For the love of money is a root of all kinds of evil."

It is no sin to have money. It becomes sin when money has you. You can possess money, or be possessed by money. If you make money the most important thing in your life, you will lie and cheat as a matter of course. You will take

3. 2 Timothy 3:2

advantage of the vulnerable, particularly the elderly, the poor, and children. Paul is talking here about the "love of money" as a major characteristic of humanity in the last days. And America today is obsessed with money.

People manipulate other people. They manipulate documents and business deals, all to get more money. You hear about people making crazy amounts of money, billions of dollars in a single day. During one happy twenty-minute period on a day in April of 2016, Amazon's Jeff Bezos made $4.9 billion. How's that for living in a different world? But don't envy him. Think about the future of money and the things of this world that money buys. It's all going to burn.

In Acts 8, a man named Simon the Sorcerer saw Peter and John doing miracles. He said, "Give me this power also, that anyone on whom I lay hands may receive the Holy Spirit."[4]

He's saying, "Peter, I've been watching you, and what you do is awesome. I wanna have what you've got." He had made his living as a sorcerer, but that was smoke and mirrors. Here was power with a capital "P." Simon wanted that Power because of the money he could make with it.

---

4. Acts 8:19

"But Peter said to him, 'Your money perish with you, because you thought that the gift of God could be purchased with money!'"[5]

"Your money perish with you" is not a curse, but a fact. When you perish, you lose it. You won't be taking money to heaven. It stays here, and even here it will not last.

As my old pastor, Greg Laurie, has often said, "You can't take it with you, but you can send it on ahead. And when we invest in God's kingdom, that is exactly what we're doing."

If you don't send it ahead, your money will perish with you. Your money will do no good for you in heaven if your main goal with it is to try to hold onto it while you're on earth. Job said, "Naked I came from my mother's womb, And naked shall I return there."[6]

PROUD BLASPHEMERS

As I write this, I want you to focus on both the single descriptors and the multiplied power they each have in context with the others.

"In the last days... men will be lovers of themselves, lovers of money, boasters, proud."[7] It's not hard to find

---

5. Acts 8:20
6. Job 1:21
7. 2 Timothy 3:1-2

ourselves in some of these categories. It's certainly not hard to find America in there.

In the last days, people will be the opposite of righteous. They will be "blasphemers, disobedient to parents, unthankful, unholy, unloving, unforgiving, slanderers, without self-control, brutal, despisers of good."[8]

"Blaspheme" comes from a Greek word that means to rail against others by speaking scandalously of them. At its worst, blasphemy means railing against God. That has become a popular theme in entertainment. Ever heard of the movie "Rapture-Palooza?" In that film, the hero shoots Jesus out of the sky as He's returning to earth on a white horse. Variety warned, "The last half-hour of this taxing comedy" turns "into one long would-be rape joke."

The movie features a fist fight between God and Satan — both extremely foulmouthed, and not much difference between them. Common Sense Media gave away the ending. It said, "Satan, God, and Jesus are… ultimately killed, leaving nonbelievers to live in peace."

That passes for humor in a time characterized by blasphemy.

---

8. 2 Timothy 3:2-3

WITHOUT GOODNESS

In verse 2, we see the phrase "disobedient to parents." Adam surely complained about Cain, and it's been going on ever since. So, to bring it up as a distinctive characteristic of the last days means a new level of disobedience and rebellion, a level that is out of the ordinary. America got a taste of this in the late sixties and early seventies. It's getting a new taste now. It will only get worse.

Then comes "unthankful, unholy, unloving, unforgiving."[9] The Greek words here all have the prefix "a-," meaning "without." As an example, "theist" refers to belief in God and "atheist" means "without belief in God." The scripture is speaking of a generation without certain things. It's missing key components needed for personal and societal health.

These people are not thankful, loving, holy, or forgiving. They are the opposite. Imagine living like that. Their self-centeredness makes them miserable!

Next, we see "slanderers."[10] The King James Bible translates this as "false accusers." This is more than speaking ill of others. It is blatantly lying about them.

---

9. 2 Timothy 3:2-3
10. 2 Timothy 3:3

We hear it often in the news. During political season, we hear it even more. People constantly bring accusations, true or not.

When Mitt Romney ran for president in 2012, then Senate Majority Leader Harry Reid made a terrible accusation against him. He said Romney hadn't paid taxes for 10 years. When it proved to be a blatant lie, you might expect Reid to show a little remorse. But you'd be wrong. In 2015, CNN's Dana Bash asked Reid if he had any regrets about saying such an awful thing. Reid replied, "I don't regret that at all. Romney didn't win, did he?"

The first five verses of 2 Timothy 3 are not boilerplate legalese. They read like an indictment specifically tailored to our time and place in history.

Chapter 15

SELF-CENTERED BRUTES

ALL THE DESCRIPTORS IN 2 TIMOTHY 3 work together in painting the picture. But "brutal" and "without self-control" are especially complementary. These self-centered, money-hungry creatures will come to have no "self-control." Then things get "brutal."

TV and film heroes regularly entertain our society by losing control and going into fits of vengeance. I talk to people, even some believers, who seem proud of their tempers, proud of those times when they lose control. But for those who know Christ, losing control is a symptom of spiritual illness. Galatians 5:22 describes "self-control" as a "fruit of the Spirit."

Losing self-control leads to fits of brutality. I mentioned that films, television shows, video games, and music are among America's chief exports. The protagonists in these entertainments, even if they are generally "good guys," regularly lose control. Anger overwhelms them and they hit, shoot, or lash out verbally. Maybe the writers see it as a sort of fantasy fulfillment, or maybe their worlds are full of such rage.

Brutality fills all forms of entertainment, even music and games. And from America, it goes everywhere. Children are brutal to other children. Gangs are brutal to communities. Terrorists are brutal to everyone. Husbands are brutal to wives, and vice-versa. We see a terrible epidemic of parents being brutal to their children. The pornography industry may claim to be about love, but it is really about brutality.

"Loss of self-control" and "brutal" translate into crimes and sins of all sorts. They each make the other worse. Brutality without inner restraint makes brutality even more severe. And loss of self-control unleashes more brutality.

Not long ago in Nebraska, a 76-year-old woman was punched and mugged… in church. Police found two suspects. Imagine this woman just standing there in church with nobody around. Somebody comes in and beats her up. And here's the horrible part. This is not an anomaly. It's happening all over the country.

"Despisers of good" … "brutal" … "no self-control." Just go down the list. We see in our time and in our country the very things that characterized the days of Noah. Brutal despisers of what is good. No restraint. Crimes of all sorts. Sin runs rampant.

No wonder more than 40,000 new laws go on the books every year in the United States.[1] We try to get people under control, but can't write laws fast enough.

Then comes "despisers of good."[2] What a horrible description of a human being — not only fail to be good, but to despise goodness itself. These brutal, self-centered human beings who lack self-control also despise goodness. And that is a recipe for disaster.

TRAITORS

2 Timothy 3:4 says men will be "traitors." They will sell each other out because they are lovers of themselves and lovers of money. The old verities like truth and honor will no longer hold sway. The word for traitor means betray. Even today, America's leaders seem willing to betray the country's best interest if it means even a temporary polit-ical gain, or contribution. They come into office swearing to protect and defend the Constitution at all costs, but they betray it.

---

1. Per the National Conference of State Legislatures
2. 2 Timothy 3:3

Verse 4 goes on to say they will be "headstrong, haughty, lovers of pleasure rather than lovers of God." Headstrong means that, despite all their flaws, they will act with obstinate certainty, and without humility. They will act rashly. "Haughty" means "to inflate with self-conceit."

"Lovers of pleasure" means exactly that. It speaks to indulging the senses. It's happening now with increasing frequency. On Easter Sunday of 2016, a Utah mother indulged her senses with methamphetamine while in the next room four men abused her nine-year-old daughter.

One week later in Pennsylvania, a toddler stood outside in the snow trying to get in the house while his mother relaxed inside with a stash of drugs. Stories where a parent grossly neglected his or her child to indulge in sensual pleasures are legion. Sadly, they happen every day.

We live in a generation of "lovers of pleasure rather than lovers of God." Why? Go back to the beginning of the list of things that make these times perilous. It began in verse two with, "men will be lovers of themselves." Who is number one? Society says over and over in a thousand different ways — you are! Books, films, talk shows and thousands of advertising messages teach it every day.

Perfumes are called "Euphoria," "Obsession," "Pink Sugar," "Gucci Guilty," "Opium," "Black Opium,"

"Passion," "Insolence," "Poison," "Hypnotic Poison," "Nude," "Narcisse," "Unforgivable," "Dior Addict," "Pure Poison," "Forbidden Euphoria," and "Tabu." If you use one of these, you probably picked it because you like how it smells, not because it sounds like the word, "taboo." But the connection to sin, danger, addiction, and adultery in their marketing is undeniable.

In the natural order of things, parents lay down their lives for their children. But in today's America, vast numbers of parents won't even lay down their weed.

To live among a proud, brutal, traitorous, headstrong, and self-centered population is to live in perilous times. When people betray God, friends, children, parents, and country, it affects everything. Authorities can't build prisons fast enough. Crime and debauchery fill the nation's streets, entertainments, and minds.

We become vulnerable to terrorists when our nation cuts off its own root system. It brings drought, fire, and famine. It happens when we betray our children by celebrating sin.

But if you speak against these things, look out. You are an evil person. You are a "hater." Planned Parenthood can cut through a dead baby's face to get his intact brain, but the person who speaks out against it is the hater.

Through Isaiah, the Lord said, "Woe to those who call evil good, and good evil."[3]

"RICH" AND "WRETCHED"

2 Timothy 3:5 completes the description with the phrase, "Having a form of godliness but denying its power."

This is spirituality without God. "I love God in my way. You love God in your way." I've had such words thrown at me many times over the years. "Well, I'm really happy that you've found your god." That type of thing. "I'm not Jewish…" "I'm not Christian…" I'm not this, I'm not that. "But I'm a very spiritual person."

Does spiritual mean you burn incense when you smoke dope? Does it mean you see yourself as intuitive, or attuned to an unseen realm? What does it mean?

Many "forms of godliness" will be admired in the last days. For some, it will even mean regular church attendance. Several New Testament passages speak to people who identify with a church, but do not belong to Christ. The best examples may be in the churches Jesus addressed in the 2nd and 3rd chapters of Revelation. Clearly, some in those churches had never accepted His salvation.

They deny the power of the Holy Spirit, and the power of the name of Jesus. They deny the truth. They do not

3. Isaiah 5:20

love the truth. If that's you, please do not confuse God's patience with His approval. Eventually, He gives such people up to the lie they cherish above Him.

2 Thessalonians 2:9-12 says, "The coming of the lawless one[4] is according to the working of Satan, with all power, signs, and lying wonders, and with all unrighteous deception among those who perish, because they did not receive the love of the truth, that they might be saved. And for this reason God will send them strong delusion, that they should believe the lie, that they all may be condemned who did not believe the truth but had pleasure in unrighteousness."

The last of the churches Jesus addressed in Revelation 3 was the church of Laodicea. With the others, His message contained at least some commendation. But He had none for Laodicea. His message to them was a call to repentance. Yes, they were spiritual, but they didn't belong to Him.

> "I know your works, that you are neither cold nor hot. I could wish you were cold or hot. So then, because you are lukewarm, and neither cold nor hot, I will vomit you out of My mouth. Because you say, 'I am rich, have become wealthy, and have need of nothing' — and do

---

4. The Antichrist

> not know that you are wretched, miserable,
> poor, blind, and naked — I counsel you to buy
> from Me gold refined in the fire, that you may
> be rich; and white garments, that you may be
> clothed, that the shame of your nakedness may
> not be revealed; and anoint your eyes with eye
> salve, that you may see." — Revelation 3:15-18

They were into the church stuff. They had money and wealth. But they didn't know the Lord. So, the Lord said, "I will vomit you out of my mouth."

These are strong words — a graphic picture of how Jesus feels about those who have a form of godliness, but deny the power thereof.

DISORGANIZED VERSUS ORGANIZED

Satan is more spiritual than any human being in the world. Of course, he is. He's a spirit being who lives in the spirit world.

Satan has a form of godliness. Of course, he does. He is his own god.

Not only is he a very spiritual person, but he really hates organized religion — or at least he hates organized believers in Christ, otherwise known as the Church. He hates it when we're organized because when we're organized we're able to get things done.

When Americans say they don't like "organized religion," they usually mean they don't like church. But it's like a race car driver saying he hates organized engines — as if they're better if they're scattered all over the room. The parts to that race car engine have no power at all until they're organized — fit together in the correct way.

When the poor need feeding, believe me, disorganized religion will not get the job done. When you have a sick loved one, and need people to take shifts at the hospital, you don't need a "random act of kindness." You need an organized group of people behind you.

When your teenager is running with the wrong crowd, you want a place for her to go that will help you guide her back onto the right track. That means you want an organization with a plan for helping and ministering to young people.

Organized, organization, and organism are all related words. The last one, "organism," is a living thing. To kill it, tear it apart. Make it "disorganized." The Church, founded and led by Jesus Christ, is also a living thing, an organism. A disorganized organism is dead.

Look at it from Satan's point of view. Why would he prefer disorganized religion? Because he sees us as the army of his Enemy. Organized, working together, we are a powerful force for good. Disorganized, disjointed, and uncoordinated, we have no power and he can easily defeat us.

The devil wants us to have "a form of godliness" while "denying its power."

LIVING IN PERILOUS TIMES

For obvious reasons, Americans don't want to face the precariousness of the situation the Bible tells us we've entered. But from sea to shining sea, America is awash in people who have been given over to the lusts of their darkened and foolish hearts.[5] According to Romans 1, that puts this nation in grave danger.

Those who rejoice at the removal of God from our schools, universities, and government functions have no idea what they've done. They've ripped holes in the dikes, compromised the integrity of the dams, and removed the levees… as a Category 5 hurricane approaches from just beyond the horizon.

"Know this, that in the last days perilous times will come."[6]

Things will get worse, but the days of peril have already arrived. 2 Thessalonians 2:7 says, "For the mystery of

5. Romans 1:21, 24
6. 2 Timothy 3:1

lawlessness is already at work; only He who now restrains will do so until He is taken out of the way."

Americans who believe they want a world without restraints don't know what they're asking for. But they will. God will do what they want. He will remove the One who restrains. After the Rapture when Jesus takes His Church into heaven, the Holy Spirit will cease to restrain evil on earth in the way He does today. Can you imagine what it will be like? We already see perilous times, but when the Church leaves, it's going to get much worse.

Chapter 16

DAYS OF SODOM

WE LOOKED EARLIER AT JESUS comparing the time near His return to the time of Noah. He also likened the last days to the days of Lot, the nephew of Abraham who lived in the town of Sodom.

"Likewise as it was also in the days of Lot: They ate, they drank, they bought, they sold, they planted, they built; but on the day that Lot went out of Sodom it rained fire and brimstone from heaven and destroyed them all. Even so will it be in the day when the Son of Man is revealed."[1]

The days of Lot were a time of extreme violence and sexual immorality. Homosexuality and rape became normal. Society not only accepted, but promoted evil. Rape gangs roving through the city had come to seem like business as usual. They either did not know, or did not care that their sin was ripening them for judgment.

---

1. Luke 17:28-30

In Genesis 19:24, judgment fell. "The Lord rained brimstone and fire on Sodom and Gomorrah, from the Lord out of the heavens."

GOD OUR JUDGE

Jonathan Edwards, the great evangelist, pastor, and theologian, said, "Men may refuse subjection to God as a Lawgiver. They may shake off the yoke of His laws by rebellion. Yet they cannot withdraw themselves from His judgment. Although they will not have God for their lawgiver, yet they shall have Him for their Judge."

God held the people of Sodom responsible for what they knew and what they should have known. But they knew very little compared with what we know, or have easy access to, and should know.

Jesus sent His disciples out into the towns and villages of Israel with a message from Him. He warned that things would be bad for the places that rejected His message — even worse than it had been for Sodom.

> Now whatever city or town you enter, inquire who in it is worthy, and stay there till you go out. And when you go into a household, greet it. If the household is worthy, let your peace come upon it. But if it is not worthy, let your

> peace return to you. And whoever will not receive you nor hear your words, when you depart from that house or city, shake off the dust from your feet. Assuredly, I say to you, it will be more tolerable for the land of Sodom and Gomorrah in the day of judgment than for that city! — Matthew 10:11-15

The name Sodom is synonymous with reprehensible sin and rebellion against God. So, why would judgment be worse for some sedate Judean village where people happened to reject the message brought to them by disciples of Jesus? Because the people of Sodom did not have God's word, and they certainly didn't have the Good News brought by the Lord's disciples — news that the long-expected Redeemer had come.

MUCH HAS BEEN GIVEN

In America, God's word is rarely out of reach. A 2006 issue of *The New Yorker* said, "The familiar observation that the Bible is the best-selling book of all time obscures a more startling fact: the Bible is the best-selling book of the year, every year. Calculating how many Bibles are sold in the United States is a virtually impossible task, but a conservative estimate is that in 2005 Americans purchased some twenty-five million Bibles—twice as many as the most recent Harry Potter book. The amount spent annually on Bibles has been put at more than half a billion dollars."

According to research by the Barna Group, 88% of Americans have at least one copy of the Bible in their homes. Most have more than one, and almost a quarter of American homes have five or more. Anyone with a smart phone, tablet, or computer with internet access can reach any version of the Bible they want at any time, plus any number of commentaries and sermons.

Johannes Gutenberg invented the printing press in 1440. The first book printed was the Bible. For a long time, even after this world-changing invention, books of any kind remained precious and few. Although Guttenberg's process brought the price down dramatically, his Bibles cost the equivalent of about three years' wages for the average clerk. Even at that price, he couldn't print them fast enough to meet demand.

At one time, the Catholic Church made itself an obstacle to ordinary people getting and reading the Bible in their own languages. John Wycliffe and his followers were known as "Bible men." They made an English translation of the Bible that heavily influenced the later King James Bible. Wycliffe's insistence that the Bible was the ultimate authority in the life of the Christian outraged the Roman church. Forty-three years after his death, on the Pope's orders, officials dug up his remains, burned them, and cast his ashes into the River Swift.

The Bible has been the most outlawed book in world history, and its readers the most persecuted. Even today, it must be smuggled into certain nations. Despite all that, it survives as the most widely read and influential book of all time.

The word of God has never been so easily accessible as it is today. It is ubiquitous for anyone who looks. In addition to Bible reading, we can receive Bible teaching on radio and television, in books, magazines, video games, plays, paintings, sculpture, and through the internet in thousands of ways. It's everywhere.

Now think again of the verse we looked at in the very beginning of this book. Luke 12:48 — "For everyone to whom much is given, from him much will be required."

When the disciples carried the message of Jesus into the towns and villages of Israel, they carried something the people of Sodom never knew. For that reason, they were held to a higher standard. And if they were held to a higher standard, what about us?

God's complete counsel is available to Americans as to no other nation, ever. The warning of Jesus should be strong in our ears. "…more tolerable for… Sodom and Gomorrah… than for that city."

WEALTH AND DECADENCE

Not long ago, San Francisco stepped up its poop patrols. I don't mean to gross you out, but humanity running wild will do gross things. When I mentioned "without self-control" you may not have thought of it in this way. San Francisco's problem represents the human condition in the last days. Do not go barefoot in a major city's downtown area. Along with the poop, vomit, and blood, the streets are filled with knives, needles, and soiled underwear.

To some, these are great times in the Bay Area. Paragon Real Estate Group reported, "San Francisco median house sales price soars to $1,500,000 in May (of 2017)." That's almost eight times the national average. Could you settle for a 488-square foot home? It'll cost you $549,000 as of August 2017. How about 811-square feet for $1.2 million?

All this shows what a booming economy they have in "the city by the bay," and in nearby Silicon Valley. So, while the rich get richer, the city's middle class can't even buy a home. Nearby Palo Alto announced it would study a proposal to give housing subsidies to people making up to $250,000 a year.

The San Francisco housing bubble has grown to such proportions because of the cash-rich tech industries centered there. Even with all that money, though, it's a perilous time to be walking the streets. Financially, things are booming. But the streets are filled with the stench of approaching death.

A *Guardian* story on the Bay Area housing bubble featured a man identified only as "Michael." He said, "You are literally stepping over people to get to your job to make hundreds of thousands of dollars."[2]

According to *The Guardian,* Michael makes $700,000 a year, but must commute 2 ½ hours to work because he can't afford to buy a decent size home any closer. He said, "We went to an open house in Los Gatos that would shorten my commute by eight miles. It was 1,700 square feet and listed at $1.4 million. It sold in 24 hours for $1.7 million."

If it's hard for him, imagine what it's like for teachers, firefighters, police, and other people with essential, but more ordinary jobs.

A 2015 Gizmodo article came with the headline, "SF's Infrastructure Is Falling Apart Because People Keep

2. "Scraping by on six figures? Tech workers feel poor in Silicon Valley's wealth bubble" by Olivia Solon, The Guardian, February 27, 2017

Peeing On It." They were not kidding. They cited examples of light poles falling over because San Franciscans so often used the base of them as a place to urinate. Over time, this causes so much corrosion that the structure fails. Gizmodo said, "Public urination is such a problem that the city's utilities commission is mounting a visual check of all 25,000 streetlights."[3]

Other parts of the city's infrastructure are failing for the same reason. This most glamorous and prosperous of American cities has become a public urinal. And it's not just disgusting. It's symptomatic. It's an outward expression of inner corruption.

That's just one American city, but the rest of America is following along. It's even worse in Great Britain where the press regularly laments the massive levels of public drunkenness on the streets of London.

Jesus said that the last days would be like the days of Noah and of Lot. It's happening, but Americans have a hard time seeing it because it has come to seem normal.

3. "SF's Infrastructure Is Falling Apart Because People Keep Peeing On It" by Alissa Walker, Gizmodo, August 5, 2015

Chapter 17

LAWLESSNESS

THROUGH MOST OF THE 24TH CHAPTER of Matthew, Jesus was answering the question, "What will be the sign of Your coming, and of the end of the age?"[1] In verse 12, Jesus said, "Because lawlessness will abound, the love of many will grow cold."

In America today, lawlessness does abound. It goes hand in hand with the phrase "perilous times." What can be more perilous than times of lawlessness? Judges 17:6 describes the chaos of lawlessness. It says, "In those days there was no king in Israel; everyone did what was right in his own eyes."

LAWLESS AMERICA

I mentioned earlier the states that have chosen to ignore federal law on the use of marijuana. But that hardly scratches the surface of lawlessness in America.

---

1. Matthew 24:3

In the last few years, we saw U.S. Justice Department officials ignore laws they didn't like. Instead of following the constitutional path of allowing the legislature to make or remove laws, certain previous Attorney Generals chose which laws to enforce based political expediency and their own whims.

Increasing lawlessness is more than a matter of rising crime statistics. It's a deterioration of respect for law at every level.

Sadly, in recent years, one of the chief criminal organizations is government itself. Not only did the Justice Department ignore certain laws, it also officially urged local law enforcement entities to ignore laws that the federal authorities didn't like. In March of 2016, the *New York Post* reported, "Attorney General Loretta Lynch has issued a warning to municipal and state judges across the country that their courts could lose federal funding if they don't ease up on fines and arrest warrants for minor crimes involving poor offenders, indigent minorities in particular."[2]

This is almost unthinkable. The highest law enforcement officer in the land, the Attorney General, threatened local judges, prosecutors, and others. She told them that if

---

2. "AG Loretta Lynch wants to let nation break law without consequences" by Paul Sperry, New York Post, March 27, 2016

they do as they have sworn to do — uphold the law — the federal government would withhold funds.

ILLEGAL IMMIGRATION

Disregard for law is happening at all levels of government. I'm totally for immigration, but not for government-sponsored lawlessness. Sanctuary cities like San Francisco flaunt federal immigration laws. Until recently, federal officials told members of the Border Patrol to apprehend people crossing the border illegally, then let them go. Catch and release. Catch them to make the apprehension statistics look good, then let them go.

Eric Shawn, Senior Correspondent Fox News Channel, reported during the Obama Administration, "Agents are under orders from the agency headquarters in Washington to release illegals by not giving them what's called NTAs, notice to appear summonses, that should send them straight to a deportation judge."

Art Del Cueto is a Border Patrol agent and Vice President of the National Border Patrol Council. He said that when illegals don't receive NTAs, "They get released back into the United States. They walk out the front door."

National Border Patrol Council Spokesman and Border Patrol agent Shawn Moran said, "We don't know who we're releasing, and we don't know what they're capable of…. You can't find out they've murdered. You can't find out if they've molested minors. You can't find out if they've raped."

For the U.S. Department of Homeland Security to order its own Border Patrol Agents to break U.S. law was the height of lawlessness — government lawlessness.

A story broke in Twin Falls, Idaho, about a possible rape case involving Muslim immigrants. The U.S. Attorney for Idaho, Wendy Olson, threatened the citizens of Twin Falls with prosecution for even talking about the case. She said, "The spread of false information or inflammatory or threatening statements about the perpetrators or the crime itself reduces public safety and may violate federal law."

"Inflammatory… statements" can mean anything. In other words, she was threatening to prosecute people for simply disagreeing with her. That again is government lawlessness.

GOVERNMENT OF LAWS AND NOT MEN

In January of 1776, Thomas Paine wrote, "In America the law is king. For as in absolute governments the King is law, so in free countries the law ought to be king; and there ought to be no other."

Our second President, John Adams, often wrote about "a government of laws and not of men." He eventually made the phrase a permanent part of the Massachusetts Constitution.

President Obama took a different approach. He changed the Affordable Care Act, sometimes known as Obamacare, 24 times. He changed it unilaterally. The Obama Administration wrote the law, then found it impossible to follow. So, they changed it without going to Congress and asking for it to be changed. I'm sorry, but that's lawlessness.

The IRS targeted conservative nonprofit groups because of their political positions. That's against the law. The Justice Department then broke the law by turning a blind eye to the lawbreakers at the IRS — again for political reasons, and against the law.

Seventy-five percent of Americans believe there is widespread government corruption. At every turn, lawlessness abounds. The whole system, people say, is guilty.

I saw a cartoon some time ago. There are versions of it all over the internet, but I could find no attribution. Whoever drew it makes the point I've been talking about. A man sits in an easy chair, and a boy has just entered the room. "Dad," the boy says, "I'm considering a career in organized crime." The father answers, "Would that be government or private sector?"

Donald Trump was elected to office saying he would drain the swamp. But this swamp does not want to be drained. We will see what happens.

DRENCHED IN CORRUPTION

The private sector is working hard to keep up with government lawlessness. Volkswagen acted in a lawless way when it programmed certain diesel engines to turn on their emissions controls only while hooked up to laboratory monitors. The software tweak gave the engines great emissions numbers while in the lab, and much more power in the real world. Automotive writers were amazed that VW had accomplished such an amazing level of clean exhaust and power. But it wasn't a technological miracle. It was a technological cheat.

Many accuse the German government of knowing about it all along. The auto industry represents the largest industry sector in Germany, and Volkswagen is the biggest of all German auto companies. You can see why so many suspect that the government tried to sweep the whole thing under the rug.

Thirty or forty years ago, several polls asked high school students if they had ever cheated on a test. The poll results horrified American adults. They learned they had raised a generation of cheaters. Today, those kids are running the world. Is it any surprise that lawlessness characterizes our time?

The Educational Testing Service (ETS) says that "In the past it was the struggling student who was more likely to cheat just to get by. Today it is also the above-average college bound students who are cheating."[3]

The above-average college bound students are the ones who'll soon be running the world.

ETS also says, "73% of all test takers, including prospective graduate students and teachers agree that most students do cheat at some point. 86% of high school students agreed.... Cheating no longer carries the stigma that it used to. Less social disapproval coupled with increased competition for admission into universities and graduate schools has made students more willing to do whatever it takes to get the A."

That means the doctor, lawyer, or other professional you turn to in a time of crisis, may not have reached his or her position through hard work, but crafty cheating.

---

3. "Academic Cheating Fact Sheet," the Educational Testing Service, 1999

LAWLESSNESS WITHOUT BORDERS

With cheating on the rise in schools, we can expect lawlessness to keep on growing from within. But it's worth noting that lawlessness is also assaulting nations from the outside. Terrorist organizations spread lawlessness with their propaganda throughout much of the world.

The breakdown of Europe's borders is also creating lawlessness of all kinds. In the early morning hours of New Year's Day, 2016, marauding bands of Middle Eastern migrant thugs, rampaged through the town of the town of Cologne, Germany. They groped, robbed, and in some cases raped more than 1200 German women. As police tried to arrest one migrant, he taunted them saying, "I am Syrian. I must be handled in a friendly manner. Mrs. Merkel invited me here!"

BLUE LIVES

Romans 13:1-4 says, "Let every soul be subject to the governing authorities. For there is no authority except from God, and the authorities that exist are appointed by God. Therefore, whoever resists the authority resists the ordinance of God, and those who resist will bring judgment on themselves. For rulers are not a terror to good works, but to evil. Do you want to be unafraid of the authority? Do what is good, and you will have praise from the same. For he is God's minister to you for good."

The Living Bible translates "governing authorities" as "the policeman." It's interesting to think of a police officer as "God's minister to you for good," but it's true. At the time those words were written, governing authorities tended to be more evil and more corrupt than similar authorities today. IRS agents aren't allowed to pocket part of the money they get from you, but tax collectors did that in those days.

Are there problems with police? Yes, and in a moment, I'll talk about that. But first I want to address a hatred for police that is so deep, and so pervasive that it cripples society's chances for justice, and individuals' chances for success.

When anarchy reigns, everyone loses.

Few things frighten most people like the thought of a revolution against police. They picture society at the hands of roving gangs of killer-rapists who take what they want by brute force. Remove the police, and that's what you get.

Revolts against police fuel fears of lawlessness. Such uprisings don't usually push a society toward anarchy, as you might expect. They push it in the opposite direction —toward a police state. People will put up with almost anything rather than see their families made vulnerable to everything.

POLICING THE POLICERS OF THE POLICE

I love and appreciate our police. They tend to be highly motivated, and extremely professional individuals doing a job that gets more difficult as the times become more perilous. I don't want to say a disparaging word about them.

But they must hire from the same labor pool as everyone else. The Equal Employment Opportunity Commission reports that, "Nearly one-third of American adults have been arrested by age 23." That either cuts into the potential labor pool for police departments, or those departments find themselves lowering standards. Most law enforcement agencies admit that over time they have done just that. They have lowered standards on things ranging from prior illegal drug use to misdemeanor convictions.

As more people become proud, blaspheming, traitorous, unholy, unforgiving, slanderers, without self-control, brutal, etc., the law enforcement officer's job becomes ever more challenging. At the same time, more and more brutal, money-lovers without self-control will slip into the ranks of the police.

If you're a member of law enforcement, believe me, I don't mean to put you down. Some of you work in departments where everyone is above reproach. But others know exactly what I'm talking about. You know officers you would never want to arrest you, or even give you a ticket. At best, they are jerks. At worst, they are criminals.

So far, the bad apples remain extremely few, and good people work hard every day to root them out. But they're there. If morals continue to decline, there will inevitably be more of them.

MORE SIN, MORE LAWS

The more unlawful people become, the more laws governments impose to keep people safe. It's a vicious cycle.

Earlier, I mentioned the number of laws enacted each year as government tries to cope with increasing lawlessness. According to the National Conference of State Legislatures, "In 2011, all 50 states and territories met in regular session and enacted more than 40,000 new bills and resolutions on issues across the board."

That's one year. There's no reason to believe it was an anomaly. And it only includes state and territorial governments — not city councils and not the federal government. Most important, it doesn't include the state and federal bureaucracies. Those are the people who create the regulations that decide how a law touches the people. A new law can contain as little as a single sentence. Federal regulators may then write hundreds or thousands of pages to explain how the law works.

In 2010, Congress passed a law officially known as the Affordable Care Act, but more commonly known as Obamacare. It was 2700 pages long. That's one reason so many in Congress didn't really read it. It was just too long. But a year later, the regulations explaining how that law works in the real world had grown to the 20,000-page range. These are pages printed with small type, and little white space. This is the way laws grow over time even when legislatures pass nothing new.

No one, not even the government, can keep up. Are these laws evil? They can be. But they are often just an attempt to solve a problem. Most of our problems are a result of human sin. We need ever more regulation because we keep finding ways to get around the old ones. The notion that no one can legislate morality carries some truth, but the whole point of human government is to try to codify right and wrong. When a nation falls under the curse of Romans 1, it can't make laws fast enough to keep up with the evil growing in the hearts of human beings.

All of this points to a society in decay and subject to the judgment of God.

Chapter 18

NATION AGAINST NATION

WHEN GIVING THE SIGNS of His return, Jesus also said, "Nation will rise against nation, and kingdom against kingdom."[1]

The Greek word translated "nation" is "ethnos." Notice the similarity to our word, "ethnic." "Ethnos" means tribe or people group. When Jesus said, "kingdom against kingdom," He meant what we call countries. But when he said, "Nation will rise against nation," it was a warning that people would tend to divide according to ethnicity.

Easy transportation and global commerce have given a cosmopolitan flavor to vast portions of the world. Practically all major cities around the globe have diverse populations. Because of this, people group rising against people group has the potential to rip those cities apart. We clearly see such divisions forming in Europe, and we're beginning to see them in America.

---

1. Matthew 24:7

Let me add here that this should never happen within the Church. We, of all people, should treat every person with the dignity and respect due to fellow creatures made in God's image, and for whom Christ died. We who believe the Bible know well the words of Acts 17:26. "He has made from one blood every nation of men to dwell on all the face of the earth."

Our family in Christ extends around the world and includes people of every ethnic background. In putting us together, God performs a miracle of love. Ephesians 2:14 says, "For He Himself is our peace, who has made both one, and has broken down the middle wall of separation."

WHAT EVERYONE LONGS FOR

Here again, people want the fruit of the Gospel, but not the Gospel itself. They want brotherhood. They want kind and gentle relationships based on mutual love and profound respect, as opposed to people using and manipulating one another for selfish gain. They want human rights and human dignity.

They want the fruit of the Spirit, so long as they don't have to have the Spirit Himself. They want the top of the tree to live even as they cut off the tree's roots.

They want the human family to extend across ethnic lines. They want Christian-like love and fellowship among all people, but they want it while simultaneously rejecting the God from Whom such love springs.

Americans have something wonderful working in their favor on this. The nation's institutions have largely discarded the knowledge of God, but vast portions of the American people have had personal encounters with Christ. He changed their lives. That is invaluable to race relations in the United States. It may be enough to hold our disparate nation together, but only until the Rapture.

EUROPEAN DISASTER

Europe is a different story. They have largely abandoned faith in Christ. They have nothing with which to stabilize the growing rifts between people groups. The nations on that continent are dynamic and shifting like fault lines before an earthquake. For decades, they imported Muslims from the Middle East to serve as their day laborers. Then came the Syrian civil war and millions more Middle Eastern Muslims poured into the region.

In such a mass migration, how can anyone know who will come in and what their goals will be? There's no way to vet people. Are they jihadists? Are they from ISIS, Hezbollah, or al-Qaeda? Earlier I mentioned the horrors in Cologne. That was just one place, in one country, on one night. We see chaos increasing across the Eurozone.

According to the United Nations, 62% of the migrants traveling to Europe in 2015 were men. *62%!* Most of these men were young. Why didn't they stay and fight against the terrorists? ISIS has stated that it has infiltrated this mass migration using it as a cover for invasion.

Even in this chaos, though, God works. In ISIS, Muslims are confronting Islam's darker side, often for the first time. It's waking many of them up. Churches in Europe report large numbers of the migrants coming to Christ. Away from home, habits, and family pressure, many are open to the Gospel for the first time.

These are exciting times for Christian witness, and it's not limited to Europe. Record numbers of Muslims are also coming to Christ in the Middle East and elsewhere.

Wonderful as this is, none of it helps western governments vet the mass of migrants. What Jesus said would happen is happening. People groups are rising against one another. We see it in Europe now, and it's growing in America.

CHANGING TIMES

The United States has long been the cultural melting pot of the world. But as we get closer to the last days, there is less melting. It's a pot with a lot of different groups, but with fewer joining the whole. Earlier immigrants came here, and within a generation or two, embraced the traditions that make America great. At the same time, they brought their own uniqueness to the overall culture. Now there is more of a tendency to stay separate. This, too, will get worse.

Nation rising against nation, in America, means Americans rising against Americans. By its nature, America is anything but racially homogenous. Civil unrest continues to increase, and only the Gospel can fix it.

With the rise in lawlessness, Americans have grown deeply frustrated. Many identify with Solomon's despair when he wrote in Ecclesiastes, "That which is crooked cannot be made straight: and that which is wanting cannot be numbered."[2]

The attitude seems to be, "There are too many problems. I can't fix them all. So, I'll just see how much fun I can have." Solomon tried this too. "Whatever my eyes desired I did not keep from them. I did not withhold my heart from any pleasure... And indeed all was vanity and grasping for the wind."[3]

The overwhelming nature of the problems gives many an excuse to simply do what is "right in his own eyes."[4]

---

2. Ecclesiastes 1:15
3. Ecclesiastes 2:10-11
4. Judges 21:25

CONTRAST

Have you ever noticed when watching a movie, that streets often look wet even when there's no rain or sign of precipitation? The people in Hollywood do this because moisture darkens and adds a sheen of reflectiveness to the asphalt. It makes the colors in the rest of the scene "pop."

Darkness makes light "pop."

As I write this, the latest buzzword in television monitors is not a word, but the acronym "HDR." It stands for "High Dynamic Range." Until recently, it was a photographic technique, but television manufacturers have made it their own with standards established by the UHD Alliance of manufacturers.

The standards include a variety of specifications, but the big one is "Contrast." It's talking about the difference between the brightest brights and the darkest darks. In a few years, people may forget this, but today when we see an HDR TV, we find it stunning. We've had "high definition" for a while, and for most people, it's old hat. But when you see a nighttime city scape on an OLED or other HDR TV, it takes your breath away.

Why? In video, contrast is the difference between darkness and light. Great contrast is the key to eye-popping video, but until now, video standards could not achieve great contrast.

These are dark days, but the darker the darkness, the more breathtaking the light. In these days, the Gospel of Jesus stands out in an ultra HD, HDR-like brilliance because the level of contrast with the world system is great, and growing greater. It makes an amazing opportunity for witness.

Chapter 19

GLOOM, DOOM AND GLORY

I DON'T LIKE GLOOM AND DOOM. No sane person does. I prefer to talk about God's love and grace, rather than His coming judgment — though they are inextricably linked. I also like warm, sunny weather. Does that mean I want the weatherman to tell me it will be a sunny day when all the signs point to a blizzard? No. I can't be prepared if those who know the truth don't warn me. And I need to be prepared.

With the judgment of God looming over America, those who claim to speak for God must sound a warning. Real love demands it.

Many to Serve; One to Please

Someone said, "The truth is kinder than kindness." Preachers and pastors, like everyone else, want to say things that people will enjoy. That usually works out well because the Bible is full of wonderful news. But ministries are not businesses. Seeing people as customers to be pleased endangers a ministry's purpose for being. We must not try to please the audience. Instead, we must serve the congregation. We have One to please, and many to serve.

I'm sure doctors prefer telling their patients that they are cancer-free. But if a patient isn't really cancer-free, the doctor does not serve that patient by saying he is. A doctor's pleasant lie can be as fatal as a gunshot to the heart.

Ministries seem to run on money. And let's face it, telling people what they want to hear can help with fund-raising. It's easy to fall into the trap. We who preach the Gospel must remember that it is *not* our job to please people. It is our job to *serve people*, and to *please God*.

JERE-MY-O-MY-AD

The prophet Jeremiah was faithful to speak the things God spoke to him. It wasn't pleasant, and he got in a lot of trouble for it. Even today, his name is synonymous with an unpopular message. The word "Jeremiad" means "a prolonged lamentation or mournful complaint."[1]

Merriam-Webster is anything but complimentary in its assessment of the word. "Jeremiah was a naysayer," they

---

1. Dictionary.com Unabridged. Retrieved April 29, 2016 from Dictionary.com website.

wrote. "That Jewish prophet, who lived from about 650 to 570 BC, spent his days lambasting the Hebrews for their false worship and social injustice and denouncing the king for his selfishness, materialism, and inequities. When not calling on his people to quit their wicked ways, he was lamenting his own lot; a portion of the Old Testament's Book of Jeremiah is devoted to his 'confessions,' a series of lamentations on the hardships endured by a prophet with an unpopular message. Nowadays, English speakers use 'Jeremiah' for a pessimistic person and 'jeremiad' for the way these Jeremiahs carry on."[2]

Among other things, that assessment gives a good indication of how far respect for the Bible has fallen.

One of the words that has in recent decades migrated out of the Church and into frequent use in mainstream society is "judgmental." No one wants to hear that word in relationship to himself. Can you imagine a Jeremiah in our day? Talk about sounding judgmental! But it was no fun then either. He said, "I am in derision daily; Everyone mocks me."[3]

It is wrong to judge Jeremiah as judgmental. He wasn't judgmental; he was faithful. He didn't pronounce his own judgment, he faithfully warned of a coming judgment from God.

2. "Jeremiad" Merriam-Webster.com, *Merriam-Webster*
3. Jeremiah 20:7

The Book of Jeremiah singles out apostate religious leaders for its strongest criticism. In Jeremiah 2:8, God said, "The priests did not say, 'Where is the Lord?' And those who handle the law did not know Me; The rulers also transgressed against Me; The prophets prophesied by Baal, And walked after things that do not profit."

The word translated "ruler" here is translated "pastor" in the King James Version.

Jeremiah 10:21 says, "For the shepherds have become dull-hearted, And have not sought the Lord; Therefore they shall not prosper, And all their flocks shall be scattered." The King James says, "For the pastors are become brutish, and have not sought the Lord."

In Jeremiah 12:10, God said, "Many rulers have destroyed My vineyard, They have trodden My portion underfoot; They have made My pleasant portion a desolate wilderness." Here also, ruler is more literally translated "pastor" or "shepherd." The Lord is saying that religious leaders who do not know Him, minister "desolation" to those who follow them.

God sounds a fierce warning in Jeremiah 23:1. "Woe to the shepherds (or pastors) who destroy and scatter the sheep of My pasture!"

Jesus, too, reserved His most harsh criticism for hypocritical religious leaders.

AWE AND WONDER WITHOUT END

Jeremiah's story does not end in defeat, but in everlasting life. God used him to teach, heal, warn, and encourage billions of people across the centuries. More than half the present population of the world — mostly Christians, Muslims, and Jews — revere Jeremiah as a prophet. God gave him that calling before birth. Despite moments of doubt, he remained faithful to it.

> Then the word of the Lord came to me, saying: "Before I formed you in the womb I knew you; Before you were born I sanctified you; I ordained you a prophet to the nations."

> Then said I: "Ah, Lord God! Behold, I cannot speak, for I am a youth."

> But the Lord said to me: "Do not say, 'I am a youth,' For you shall go to all to whom I send you, And whatever I command you, you shall speak. Do not be afraid of their faces, For I am with you to deliver you," says the Lord.

> Then the Lord put forth His hand and touched my mouth, and the Lord said to me: "Behold, I have put My words in your mouth."
> — Jeremiah 1:4-9

God did not see Jeremiah's age as either a qualifier or a disqualifier. The bottom line was that God had chosen Jeremiah. The calling on his life would entail a great deal of pain, but it was also amazing beyond imagination. The Living God chose Jeremiah to speak for Him.

If you are in Christ, you are called to the same purpose. It will not always be easy. But it will always be astounding. It will never get old. Buy the nicest car on the lot, and you'll enjoy it. But within a few days, driving it will become ordinary — just another thing you do. But when it comes to speaking as God's ambassador[4], the wonder will never wear out.

THE ARK

Let's go back again to the words of Jesus in Matthew 24:37. "As the days of Noah were, so also will the coming of the Son of Man be."

The Bible tells us a lot about the time of Noah. The most obvious thing is this. God's judgment fell on the world. Rain descended from the skies. Waters surged up from "the great deep."[5] Water engulfed the world.

Noah's story tells us amazing things about God — starting with the fact that He holds human beings

4. 2 Corinthians 5:20
5. Genesis 7:11

accountable for their actions. He pronounces judgment, then carries it out. We should never take these facts lightly.

It doesn't matter if you disagree with God's judgment. Let's say you've been found guilty of murder in the first degree. Before pronouncing judgment, the presiding judge asks if you have anything to say for yourself. You answer that in your opinion, first degree murder should have no punishment, "and besides, lots of people do it."

Will it make any difference? If anything, your callousness will result in a harsher punishment.

The God who possesses all knowledge and all wisdom will not be swayed by the defendant's appraisal of Him or of His eternal decrees. God judges. He does so fairly, meting out perfect justice to everyone.

Noah's story tells us something else about God, and it's even more amazing! Yes, there was rain, and a flood. The judgment of God poured out onto the world. But there was also an ark — a way of escape. There was judgment, but also grace.

In *Surprised by Joy*, C. S. Lewis wrote, "The hardness of God is kinder than the softness of men, and His compulsion is our liberation."

They may call you judgmental. They may call you "a hater." But the message of Christ is always ultimately a message of love, peace, forgiveness, and redemption.

Noah spent 120 years building the ark. 2 Peter 2:5 calls Noah "a preacher of righteousness." Combine those two facts, and you get 120 years of warning and opportunity for escape. Even so, Jesus said the flood caught people by surprise. They didn't listen.

The ark was there. It was available. But the people ignored the "preacher of righteousness."

We, too, have an Ark. Our Ark is a person with a name — Jesus. In Him, and only in Him, will you find peace and security.

GRACE AT EVERY HAND

Larry Alex Taunton released a book showing a different side to the famous, and extremely outspoken atheist, Christopher Hitchens. Taunton set up debates between Christians and famous atheists, including Hitchens. The two men sometimes rode together on the long trips to these debates. During the trips, they became friends.

Despite what his critics say, Mr. Taunton does not claim in his book that Hitchens converted to Christianity on his deathbed. Rather, he claims that in private, Hitchens showed the kind of interest that sometimes leads to conversion.

On one of their road trips, Taunton drove and Hitchens read aloud from the Book of John, stopping often for discussion. "Where is grace in the Old Testament?" Hitchens asked at one point. "I see it in the New Testament, but God is different in the Old Testament."

Taunton then correctly took Hitchens to the Genesis story of Abraham, the man who "believed God, and it was accounted to him for righteousness."[6]

In fact, we find grace throughout the Old Testament. Even as God poured out His second harshest judgment on humanity so far[7] — He provided the ark. And in the ark, we see grace. God's justice was expressed in a horrible judgment — a flood. His grace was expressed with a beautiful boat — the ark.

In the cross of Christ, we find both. In it we see the flood of judgment and the security of the ark. Justice demanded judgment, so the One who is both perfectly just and perfectly loving, took that judgment on Himself.

GRACE

How did Noah and his family receive grace when everyone else received judgment? Was it his sinless perfection?

6. Romans 4:3, Genesis 15:6

7. As mentioned earlier, God's most severe judgment was the curse of death released into the world following Adam and Eve's sin in Genesis 3.

The Bible says, "No." Romans 3:10 and 23 neatly summarize Noah's predicament, along with the rest of humanity. "There is none righteous, no, not one.... All have sinned and fall short of the glory of God."

That means Noah was also a sinner. So, what made the difference? Hebrews 11:7 says that it was Noah's faith. "By faith Noah, being divinely warned of things not yet seen, moved with godly fear, prepared an ark for the saving of his household, by which he condemned the world and became heir of the righteousness which is according to faith."

Today, God is calling each of us to choose faith in Him so that, like Noah, we can receive the gift of God's own righteousness. The door is open. Judgment is falling, but our Ark awaits. Jesus stands before us with His arms open. Psalm 34:8 says, "Oh, taste and see that the Lord is good; Blessed is the man who trusts in Him!"

Chapter 20

REPENTANCE AND REPRIEVE

A MAN ARRIVED IN ONE OF THE GREAT CITIES of the world. He was not a celebrity, not a sophisticate. From what we can tell, he was not even particularly winsome, nor even kind. He had no credentials to impress the city. He probably had a somewhat weird appearance, and what he said was both frightening and strange.

But when Jonah spoke, Nineveh listened.

Jonah arrived in Nineveh having recently spent three days and nights in the belly of a great fish. Obviously, it took a miracle for him to survive down there, but the Bible gives the distinct impression that God allowed natural processes to work to some degree. So, it's easy to think of the great fish's digestive juices bleaching Jonah's hair completely white, and making his skin... well, something other than pretty.

THE BURDEN OF NINEVEH

Nineveh was an ancient city, founded by Nimrod.[1] It was for a while the largest city in the world. Several Hebrew prophets spoke God's warning to the Ninevites. Warnings in the book of Nahum are particularly strong. In 612 B.C., Nineveh was destroyed as the prophets foretold. In fact, it was so completely demolished that, for a long time, liberal scholars didn't believe the city ever existed. That changed when Nineveh's ruins began to be uncovered during 19th century excavations.

Today, not only has Nineveh's existence been confirmed, but also its size as described in the Book of Jonah. The inner city had a wall about eight miles long. The city also had extensive suburbs. Jonah 3:3 describes greater-Nineveh's size when it says, "Now Nineveh was an exceedingly great city, a three-day journey in extent."

Jonah went about the city preaching. The Bible only gives a single sentence from all that preaching, but it is a striking one. Jonah 3:4 says, "He cried out and said, 'Yet forty days, and Nineveh shall be overthrown!'"

Then something amazing happened. Nineveh repented.

Jonah 3:5-10 tells some of the things they did as expressions of their repentance, but the biggest single thing came

---

1. Genesis 10:11

at the beginning of the list. Verse 5 says, "The people of Nineveh believed God."

It's reminiscent of something found in the book of Genesis. Abraham "believed in the Lord, and He accounted it to him for righteousness."[2] It's recounted again in Romans 4:3. "Abraham believed God, and it was accounted to him for righteousness."

Jonah 3:10 says, "God saw their works, that they turned from their evil way; and God relented from the disaster that He had said He would bring upon them, and He did not do it."

Jonah's preaching was the most effective in the history of the world. An entire society turned to God *en masse*. In Matthew 12:41, Jesus would tell the people of Israel in His time, "The men of Nineveh will rise up in the judgment with this generation and condemn it, because they repented at the preaching of Jonah; and indeed a greater than Jonah is here."

Jonah repented while in the belly of the great fish, and God spared Jonah. When the people of Nineveh repented, God spared them, too.

AMERICAN MIRACLE

If America turns to God, will He spare this nation?

2. Genesis 15:6

Theologians often debate the meaning Genesis 6:3 — "And the Lord said, 'My Spirit shall not strive with man forever.'" But the story of Pharaoh in the time of Moses and of various generations of the people of Israel, shows that God does sometimes reach a place where He stops dealing in mercy with a generation.

At the same time, God is rich in mercy. His message to the people of Nineveh was a harsh one. It seemed to leave no room for redemption. In Jonah 3:4, the prophet "cried out and said, 'Yet forty days, and Nineveh shall be overthrown!'"

At first there seems to be no wiggle room. But the fact that God was giving them this warning proved that He still wanted to reach them. He went to a great deal of trouble just to get His angry, rebellious prophet to the city to deliver His message.

Has America passed the point of no return? I don't think so. He's still sending preachers forth with His word. His Holy Spirit is still convicting Americans of sin. He still hears the sinner's prayer of repentance.

In the 1970s, something called "the Jesus movement" started on the West Coast and spread across the nation. It had its flaws, and it wasn't a Nineveh-like moment. The whole country didn't turn to God. But millions did, and things changed.

I believe the Jesus movement directly led to God raising up a special group of leaders — Margaret Thatcher in the U.K., Ronald Reagan in the U.S., and Menachem Begin in Israel. With them was another man whose life took a dramatic turn in the 1970s — Anwar Sadat.

The end of the 1980s felt further from Armageddon than the end of the 1960s had. The human oppression factory known as the Soviet Union was falling apart. Israel seemed dramatically closer to peace. The world was turning more toward civil rights and human dignity.

Could it happen again? Yes. Will it? We're not yet headed in that direction, but as long as God continues to reach out to our nation, repentance remains possible. Even after judgment begins, it can be lessened by a turn to God.

In 1991, record numbers of Americans went to church the Sunday before the ground portion of Operation Desert Storm began in Iraq. No one really knew what was going to happen. Would Iraq unleash chemical weapons as it had in past conflicts? How strong were they? Politicians opposing the war warned that the Pentagon had ordered 15,000 body bags.

American lives were lost — 148 to be exact, and each one precious. Military operations should never be depicted as easy, but it was nothing like the horror that had been predicted. God answered the prayers of Americans. And Americans… promptly forgot.

Instead of thanking God, we boasted of our superior military training and technology.

ANOTHER REPRIEVE

God never fires on the nation whose hands are lifted in surrender. It was this aspect of God's nature that Jonah said turned him away from Nineveh in the first place. He was afraid that he would tell people they were on the verge of destruction, they would repent, God would give them a reprieve, and Jonah would look ridiculous.

> When God saw what they had done and how they had put a stop to their evil ways, He changed His mind and did not carry out the destruction He had threatened.

> This change of plans greatly upset Jonah, and he became very angry. So he complained to the Lord about it: "Didn't I say before I left home that You would do this, Lord? That is why I ran away to Tarshish! I knew that You are a merciful and compassionate God, slow to get angry and filled with unfailing love. You are eager to turn back from destroying people. Just kill me now,

Lord! I'd rather be dead than alive if what I predicted will not happen."

The Lord replied, "Is it right for you to be angry about this?"[3]

God's nature has not changed. He is still merciful, compassionate, and slow to anger. He still prefers to turn back from destroying people. He's eager to turn back from judgment against America.

REVIVAL

We can turn to God as a nation at any time. But I have even better news. Those of us who know the Lord don't have to wait for the media, academia, or government. Those of us who already believe can have a profound effect on the nation we love right now just by allowing Him to return us to our "first love."[4]

Great Awakenings are not one-and-done events. Another generation arises, makes its choices, and God responds. In Nineveh's case, the change created a 150-year reprieve. It could have gone on, but they again turned from God. Other generations would choose another direction.

But that does not diminish the miracle given to those who believed God in Jonah's day, and repented.

3. Jonah 3:10-4:4 NLT
4. Revelation 2:4

Chapter 21

WHEN JUDGMENT FINALLY FALLS

IN LEVITICUS 26, God describes the cycles of discipline He would bring on Israel if they broke their covenant with Him. Each cycle would be worse than the one before until finally they reached the zenith of His discipline.

> I will lay your cities waste and bring your sanctuaries to desolation, and I will not smell the fragrance of your sweet aromas. I will bring the land to desolation, and your enemies who dwell in it shall be astonished at it. I will scatter you among the nations and draw out a sword after you; your land shall be desolate and your cities waste. — Leviticus 26:31-33

We see the prophetic warning of the last cycle of discipline begin to be fulfilled when Nebuchadnezzar of Babylon besieged and defeated Jerusalem. He took

Judah's King Jehoiakim back with him to Babylon. After that, other terrible things happened, but the people did not take this final opportunity to repent.

DISASTER STRIKES

King Zedekiah "did evil in the sight of the Lord his God... He also rebelled against King Nebuchadnezzar, who had made him swear an oath by God; but he stiffened his neck and hardened his heart against turning to the Lord God of Israel. Moreover all the leaders of the priests and the people transgressed more and more, according to all the abominations of the nations, and defiled the house of the Lord which He had consecrated in Jerusalem."[1]

Although they could already see the terrible conse- quences of their evil actions beginning to occur, they would not stop. God remained slow to anger. Even in sending Nebuchadnezzar, God remained gentle. They repaid the Lord's kindness with more sin and rebellion.

2 Chronicles 36:15-16 are among the saddest verses in all the Bible. "The Lord God of their fathers sent warn- ings to them by His messengers, rising up early and send- ing them, because He had compassion on His people and on His dwelling place. But they mocked the messengers of God, despised His words, and scoffed at His prophets,

1. 2 Chronicles 36:12-14

until the wrath of the Lord arose against His people, till there was no remedy."

When "there was no remedy," the Living God took action.

> Therefore He brought against them the king of the Chaldeans, who killed their young men with the sword in the house of their sanctuary, and had no compassion on young man or virgin, on the aged or the weak; He gave them all into his hand. And all the articles from the house of God, great and small, the treasures of the house of the Lord, and the treasures of the king and of his leaders, all these he took to Babylon.
>
> Then they burned the house of God, broke down the wall of Jerusalem, burned all its palaces with fire, and destroyed all its precious possessions. And those who escaped from the sword he carried away to Babylon, where they became servants to him and his sons.
> — 2 Chronicles 36:17-21

That's the situation in which we find one of the Bible's greatest heroes — Daniel.

> Now from among those of the sons of Judah were Daniel, Hananiah, Mishael, and Azariah.

> To them the chief of the eunuchs gave names:
> he gave Daniel the name Belteshazzar; to
> Hananiah, Shadrach; to Mishael, Meshach;
> and to Azariah, Abed-Nego. — Daniel 1:6-7

Most English-speakers remember Daniel by his Hebrew name and the other three by their Chaldean names. Daniel's name is easy to say in English and it's the title of the book. Plus, the names "Hananiah, Mishael, and Azariah" just don't have the poetic panache of "Shadrach, Meshach, and Abed-Nego."

These four boys had done nothing to cause the disaster at Jerusalem, but it hit them hard. We have other examples of disaster falling on people who in no way brought it on themselves.

"MY NAME IS CHRISTINE"

A Jewish lawyer named Raphael Lemkin coined the term "genocide. He needed a word to describe the 20th century's first, and often forgotten, holocaust — the systematic extermination of the Armenian people between the years 1915 and 1923. On April 21, 1997, a bill was pending before the California Assembly that would set aside April 24th of that year as "California Day of Remembrance for the Armenian Genocide of 1915-1923."

An Assemblywoman made a speech opposing the bill. She made the absurd claim that what the Ottomans did to the Armenians did not amount to genocide. The bill's sponsor, Assemblyman Howard Kaloogian, then rose to defend his bill. At first, he spoke in general terms showing the historical and linguistic error of the dissenter. He showed that the very word "genocide" had been created to describe the Armenian disaster. Then he spoke from the heart about a little girl named Christine. She would grow up to be someone of crucial importance to him.

> Let me close by telling you what happened to my grandmother who told me the story many times. She saw her brothers and sisters and parents murdered before her. She was able to escape.
>
> A family in the neighborhood took her into their household and told her, "You will no longer be called 'Christine' because that is a Christian name and it will give you away. You will be called…" this other name — and she never revealed that other name to us. But it was a Turkish name.
>
> Think of the meaning of your name. Think of the meaning to you that your name has. To be taken away from your family, to see your family murdered, and to have your very identity

removed from you. It was a very traumatic experience for that ten-year-old.

Then she was told she was no longer a Christian, but she must be a Muslim. She was no longer an Armenian, but she is now a Turk; that she cannot speak Armenian, she must speak Turkish. And every night she would cry herself asleep and she would remind herself and she would pray to her God.

And she would say "My name is not…" this other name. "My name is Christine. I am not Turkish. I am Armenian. I am not Muslim. I am Christian. I do speak Armenian, and I will remember my language."

— Howard Kaloogian, April 21, 1997

A family, a name, a heritage, a faith, and a hope — all ripped away in a terrible and violent upheaval. That's what an Armenian girl named Christine faced in the early 20th century. That's also what Daniel and his friends faced more than 25 centuries earlier.

OUR NAME IS DANIEL

We don't know his exact age when these terrible things befell Daniel, but he was probably 12, 13, or 14-years-old.

He did not cause these calamities, but he felt the full weight of them. Like Howard Kaloogian's grandmother, he saw friends and family murdered before his eyes.

He also saw the enemy desecrate and rip apart the holiest place on earth. They tore him away from what remained of his family. They took him as a prisoner away from the land of his fathers. He would never see it again in his lifetime. Psalm 137 gives us a clue about the anguish felt by the captives.

> By the rivers of Babylon, There we sat down, yea, we wept When we remembered Zion. We hung our harps Upon the willows in the midst of it. For there those who carried us away captive asked of us a song, And those who plundered us requested mirth, Saying, "Sing us one of the songs of Zion!"
>
> How shall we sing the Lord's song In a foreign land?
>
> If I forget you, O Jerusalem, Let my right hand forget its skill! If I do not remember you, Let my tongue cling to the roof of my mouth — If I do not exalt Jerusalem Above my chief joy.
> — Psalm 137:1-6

The torment rises in the last three verses. The captives go from sad resignation to a rage for revenge.

> Remember, O Lord, against the sons of Edom
> The day of Jerusalem, Who said, "Raze it, raze
> it, To its very foundation!"
>
> O daughter of Babylon, who are to be
> destroyed, Happy the one who repays you as
> you have served us! Happy the one who takes
> and dashes Your little ones against the rock!
> — Psalm 137:7-9

God does not condone smashing babies against rocks. These are not verses on how we should respond to grief. They are here to graphically convey the anger and frustration these men and women felt when they remembered what the Babylonians had done to their families, and their beloved Jerusalem.

Daniel does not tell us his thoughts as he was bound and led away to far off Babylon. But this is the environment in which he was taken.

Today, our children face a situation remarkably similar to that faced by Daniel.

Chapter 22

GOD'S JUDGMENT AND YOUR CHILDREN

WHEN MOST CHRISTIANS CONTEMPLATE the idea of America falling under the judgment of God, they feel little or no fear for themselves. But they feel anguished dread at the thought of their children, their grandchildren, or anyone's children, caught up in the terrors to come.

If that strikes a chord with you, remember Psalm 103:17. "But the mercy of the Lord is from everlasting to everlasting On those who fear Him, And His righteousness to children's children."

God wants us to know that He cares for our children. He loves them even more than we do. To fear for them would just make them afraid. Instead, prepare them. Proverbs 22:6 famously says, "Train up a child in the way he should go, And when he is old he will not depart from it."

Prepare doesn't mean having a massive supply of beans in the basement. It means learning about the Lord and His ways. It means to study with them, sing with them, and have fun with them. Playtime, combined with loving discipline and teaching about Christ, builds character and strength into their souls.

It won't stop catastrophes, but it will give greatness the opportunity to rise out of the ashes. Just look at Daniel.

EDUCATING TO ERODE FAITH

The Chaldeans (a.k.a. Babylonians) were master conquerors. They understood that real victory was not just won on the battlefield, but in minds and hearts. Ultimately, conquering another people meant changing their thought patterns. In this sense, all wars are culture wars.

To change a people's way of thinking starts with the young. Old people are set in their ways, but they sometimes compromise their standards out of love for their changed young. Even if the old don't change, time is on the side of youth simply because older people usually die sooner.

Retraining youth means rewriting their environment. For the Babylonians, that meant moving Daniel and the others almost a thousand miles away to a new nation with different customs and a different history.

Today's culture only rarely tries to remove children from their homes physically (though they love to leave that threat hanging over Christian parents' heads). But using school and the immense array of media bombarding children, they try to defeat Judeo-Christian culture by changing the context within which the young see the world. Moving a child to a different country created an immersive new context for Daniel and his friends. Modern "Babylonians" accomplish this through entertainment and education.

BREAK 'EM DOWN

The idea was to turn Hebrews into Chaldeans — in thought, manner, philosophy, and religion. How do you do that? In the classic film *Hoosiers*, Coach Norman Dale (played by Gene Hackman) faced a similar dilemma. He was going to take a group of individual basketball players, change their way of thinking, and turn them into a basketball team. And he was not going to turn them into just any team, but *his* team. They would play basketball *his* way. At one point, he described the process in a single sentence. "I'm gonna break them down, and then I'm gonna build them back up."

Every coach understands this concept, as do drill sergeants, and even cult leaders. Don't get me wrong. Sports teams and the military are not cults. But the idea of tearing down the old person and building a new one is common across all these areas and many more.

For the Hebrews, the tearing down came with the destruction of their city, their country, temple, and families. Babylon wasn't just trying to raze Jerusalem to its foundation. They were razing the inner lives of these young people.

The message is obvious. "The old way is dead. Defeated. Destroyed. Time to turn to something new."

BUILD 'EM UP!

After everything's taken away, including the person's sense of worth and direction, that person becomes like a starving man. The first food he needs is a compliment or a kind word. Imagine having a representative of the most powerful man in the world tell you that you're handsome, wise, smart, and clever. They say that you deserve to have a stellar career at the center of the most powerful kingdom in the history of the world to that time.

Daniel 1:3-4 says, "The king instructed Ashpenaz, the master of his eunuchs, to bring some of the children of Israel and some of the king's descendants and some of the nobles, young men in whom there was no blemish, but good-looking, gifted in all wisdom, possessing knowledge and quick to understand, who had ability to serve in the king's palace, and whom they might teach the language and literature of the Chaldeans."

The palace then, would be something like the White House today. Every time America elects a new president, the transition team must sift through tens of thousands of applicants. They all want to join the new administration, and to get as close as possible to the seat of power.

The process of building up these young Israelites in the image of Babylon used a carrot and a stick. The stick was the possibility of punishment, and in Babylon at that time, punishment often meant death. The carrot was mostly flattery. It was a form of seduction, and flattery goes with seduction like ice cream goes with cones.

> "Say to wisdom, 'You are my sister,' and call understanding your nearest kin, That they may keep you from the immoral woman, from the seductress who flatters with her words."
> — Proverbs 7:4-5

Just remember, "the seductress… flatters."

NAMES

The first compliment was to tell these young men that they belonged among the world's elites. The Babylonians gave their special training only to the best and brightest. These young captives were culled away from the ordinary people. For the Babylonians, this had the added benefit of removing future leaders from conquered peoples, and perhaps preventing future rebellions. It also constantly replenished the talent pool in Babylon.

They didn't just plunder material riches from other cultures, but saw human talent as even more valuable.

Babylon was the most fantastic place in the ancient world, and wonder of wonders, they saw these boys as special. That's heady stuff for anyone, especially adolescents.

Daniel 1:7 says, "Then the commander of the officials assigned new names to them; and to Daniel he assigned the name Belteshazzar, to Hananiah Shadrach, to Mishael Meshach, and to Azariah Abed-nego." (NASB)

Today, few think much about the meaning of their names. In those days, though, it was a very big deal. "Daniel" means "God is my Judge." They changed it to, "Belteshazzar." That name carries a pagan blessing — "May Bel protect his life." Bel was the chief Babylonian god.

"Hananiah" means "Jehovah is gracious." The Babylonians called him "Shadrach." That means "illumined by the sun god." In other words, they saw Hananiah as brilliant.

"Mishael" means "Who or what the Lord is" — a powerful name that resonates with authority and mystery of the one God revealing Himself into time and space. They renamed him "Meshach." That means, "Who is Ishtar?" Ishtar was the Chaldean goddess of love, beauty, sex, desire, fertility, war, combat, and political power. Strong stuff.

"Azariah" means "the Lord is my help." They gave him the name, "Abed-nego." It means "the servant of Nego." That's a huge compliment because Nego was the god of wisdom and intelligence. It was the kind of flattery that might sweep even a mature person completely off his feet.

LANGUAGE

To remake their minds meant a new superstructure of thought. They didn't just want these young men to be able to speak and understand Chaldean, they wanted them to think in Chaldean — even to dream in Chaldean.

We call it "brain plasticity." It means that brains change according to what we choose to think about, and how we think. Brain plasticity allows people with severe brain injuries to recover because over time, the brain has the ability to rewire itself. Scientists used to think of brain plasticity mostly as a phenomenon of childhood. But while children's brains are more easily rewired than those of adults, brains remain malleable throughout life.

The Holy Spirit, of course, has always known this.

> Finally, brethren, whatever things are true, whatever things are noble, whatever things are just, whatever things are pure, whatever things are lovely, whatever things are of good report, if there is any virtue and if there is anything praiseworthy — meditate on these things.
> — Philippians 4:8

Why think on these things? There are lots of reasons, but a good one is that your thoughts physically rewire your brain. Thoughts also change the chemical balance of your brain. This isn't just spiritual, but physical.

Recent studies show that languages also rewire the brain. This is not a bad thing. It usually makes us smarter in other areas such as math and science. But it can also be a powerful brainwashing tool.

For Daniel and his friends, immersion into a new language meant identifying with a different culture. This wasn't simple classroom learning. They didn't sprinkle the new language, they believed in full immersion.

Have you ever listened to a kid talking to a friend on the phone, and you didn't seem to understand any of it? Every American subculture has its own language and its own rules of behavior.

Even Christians have come to see cursing and vulgarities as a briefly satisfying way to express feelings. But those Christians who feel that way may be making their kids vulnerable to people who will take "bad" language to new depths. Profanity opens children up to a profane worldview.

Language and thought have great influence on one another. When we emulate speech patterns of another person, even speaking our own language, we begin to mirror the speaker's mode of thought. The speaker can be the person standing before a class, a buddy you're hanging out with, or a popular singer. Within a church or other Christian community, this interchange of thought can be a powerful force for good.

We can also form harmful patterns of thought. In his 1946 essay, "Politics and the English Language," George Orwell wrote, "If thought corrupts language, language can also corrupt thought."

Change the word "corrupt" in his sentence to "influence" and you see what I mean. "If thought influences language, language can also influence thought." Language influences thought — even to the point of corruption.

Orwell also observed, "The slovenliness of our language makes it easier for us to have foolish thoughts."

The Babylonian system of immersing their brightest captives in the Chaldean language made the young people from Israel even more susceptible to the overall spiritual and cultural brainwashing of their captors. Each captive learned the Chaldean language so well that he began to think in it. This made it easier for the Babylonians to pass their thoughts, manner of thinking, and worldview to the young captives. It was part of the process of brainwashing.

POTTERSVILLE

All this is important because something similar is happening to Americans. In October of 2016, renowned prophecy teacher Hal Lindsey wrote, "We in America haven't been taken to a new country, but we have watched as a new country has formed around us."

In that sense, we're all Daniel. Or, maybe we're more like George Bailey in *It's a Wonderful Life* — suddenly transported out of Bedford Falls and into Pottersville. The America of yesterday is gone, and something terrible has taken its place.

Furthermore, this morally rotting Pottersville faces judgment from God. What do we do? What will happen to our children?

THRIVING IN POTTERSVILLE

Daniel never saw Jerusalem again in this life. For him, that was an ongoing tragedy. But he influenced the world for God. He had trials (remember the lion's den!) but with the trials, he had almost unimaginable success. He helped rule two different kingdoms. And each of those kingdoms, in their time, ruled the world.

He and his friends, Hananiah, Mishael, and Azariah, became the prototypes for a Jewish nation in diaspora. Spread across the world for millennia, they remained distinctly Jewish wherever they went. They were not assimilated, as were every comparable group in history.

Daniel showed them how remain Israelites, yet thrive in new environments. His example is valid for us, too. The formula (if we can call it that) is as simple as your earliest Sunday School lessons. First, he prayed regularly. The Book of Daniel is a book of many prayers. Daniel was thrown into the lion's den because his prayers were unabashed, systematic, and regular.

Second, Daniel was a man of the Word. Daniel 9:2 says, "I, Daniel, understood by the books the number of the years specified by the word of the Lord through Jeremiah the prophet, that He would accomplish seventy years in the desolations of Jerusalem."

He spent his time studying what we call the Book of Jeremiah. This was normal for him.

Third, Daniel was not ashamed of his faith in God. King Nebuchadnezzar was notorious for cutting off the heads of advisors who said things he didn't like. But Daniel stood up to him. Instead of telling the King what he wanted to hear, Daniel told him what he needed to hear. He told him about the one, true God. He did it often and without shame or embarrassment.

I hope you're not disappointed that my profound advice mirrors those early Sunday School lessons. But it's the truth. We need to pray, read the Bible, and tell others about God. We preachers often do our best work when we remind people of the profound things they learned in Sunday School. Here, it is the recipe for overcoming the adversity of the world.

There's one more thing to remember about Daniel. He believed God! Everything about him sprang from his faith.

The fall of Jerusalem did not shatter Daniel's faith. That's because he knew both the warnings of God and His promises. Judgment came, but that only confirmed this young man's belief in the reliability of scripture. Daniel knew that God's promises were also true, and that they applied to him.

It worked for Daniel in a time when his nation fell under the judgment of God. It will also work for us, and for our little ones.

Chapter 23

GOD'S JUDGMENT AND YOU

THEY CALLED HIM THE "Wizard of Westwood." The University of California at Los Angeles (UCLA) is located in the Westwood section of the city. The man they called the "Wizard" was anything but. He was a Christian basketball coach with a knack for teaching the ways of winning.

John Wooden coached the UCLA Bruins from 1948 to 1975. During the last twelve years of his UCLA coaching tenure, his teams won an unprecedented (and almost unimaginable) ten championships. Since 1960, five men's Division I basketball teams went undefeated. Four of them were coached by Wooden.

In 2009, *The Sporting News* named him the "Greatest Coach of All Time" — not basketball coach or college coach. Just "coach." They said he was the greatest coach in any sport you want to name. That sounds extreme, but it's not an exaggeration.

Wooden faithfully attended church, and read the Bible daily. He wrote, "I'm not a relativist. I don't think we're supposed to find our own truth. That's playing God. I believe in absolute truth and absolute sin, and the Bible is my standard for determining those absolutes."[1]

Later in the same book, he wrote, "I've trusted Christ and I've tried to live as He would have me live. I've studied His word and I've prayed a great deal. I have faith He will do what He's promised."[2]

In another book, he wrote, "I have always tried to make it clear that basketball is not the ultimate. It is of small importance in comparison to the total life we live. There is only one kind of life that truly wins, and that is the one that places faith in the hands of the Savior."[3]

LIFE LESSONS

Basketball is not ultimate, but Coach Wooden was the ultimate basketball coach. He's been imitated, but never equaled. You might imagine that he was a brilliant tactician, and you'd be right. He was an innovator. His ideas have been copied by coaches the world over.

---

1. *Coach Wooden's Pyramid of Success Playbook* by John Wooden and Jay Carty, Regal Books, 2005
2. ibid.
3. *They Call Me Coach* by John Wooden, McGraw-Hill, 1988

But that's only part of what made him the "greatest coach." For Wooden, winning started with the basics — with getting the little things right.

Through the years, his players grew to love as well as admire him, but in the 1960s and 70s, he already seemed like a relic. In truth, he would have seemed old-fashioned even if he had coached several decades earlier. Later they realized that his ways were old, but not antiquated. His approach to basketball and to life was not timeworn, but timeless.

Nothing illustrates that better than the shock his young players felt when they received their first basketball lesson from the legendary coach. He had them circle up, then sit down. "Men," he began, "this is how you put your shoes and socks on."

Bill Walton was one of the most talented and headstrong players Wooden ever coached. He was a three-time consensus All-American for UCLA, the player of the year in 1973, and UCLA never even lost a game he played in until his senior year.

With the perspective of many years, Walton wrote an autobiography. He told about the moment when he heard Coach Wooden tell them he was going teach them how to put on their shoes and socks.

We were stunned. We looked around and at each other. Are you kidding me? We're all high school All-America players and here is this silly little old man showing us how to put on our shoes and socks! ... We were rolling our eyes and could barely keep from laughing out loud. When he took off his own shoes and socks for the demo, we were appalled. He had these grotesque varicose veins covering his lower legs, feet, and ankles....

Meticulously, he demonstrated exactly how we were to apply the socks over our toes and pull them up tight to eliminate the possibility of any wrinkles, which could cause blisters. And then how to open our shoes so that they would slide on easily and not disturb the wrinkle-free socks, and how to then properly lace and tie them snuggly and completely.[4]

Walton went on to stardom in the NBA and a successful career in broadcasting. At an event honoring Wooden, he said the coach's lesson on shoes and socks was the initial lesson for "everything we would need to know for the rest of our lives."

---

4. *Back from the Dead* by Bill Walton, Simon & Schuster, 2016

A STRONG FOUNDATION

Coach Wooden knew that to succeed, we need to get the basics right. Build a good foundation. He said, "Basketball is a game that's played on a hardwood floor. And to be good, you have to… change your direction, change your pace. That's hard on your feet. Your feet are very important."

His shoe lesson was practical and symbolic. He taught his players to do the little things, the basic things, right. But he was also teaching them the practical matter of taking care of their feet — their foundation. "To be strong," he wrote, "you have to have a strong foundation."

How strong is your foundation?

STORM WARNING

In this book, I've warned of a coming storm. It may dissipate some, and not be as bad as expected. Or it may intensify. When you look at the signs all around, it might make you afraid — for yourself, for those you love, or maybe even for people you don't know.

How do you get ready? What things can you do to prepare? Start by getting your shoes and socks on. Do it carefully, but don't waste time. Coach Wooden said, "Be quick, but don't hurry."

When you hurry, you go into a frenzy. That's when boxers flail at the air. But you can only be quick without the frenzy when you know where you're going and what you're doing. You need certainty, and that's another word for faith.

In Matthew 7:24-27, Jesus illustrated the two approaches. "Whoever hears these sayings of Mine, and does them, I will liken him to a wise man who built his house on the rock: and the rain descended, the floods came, and the winds blew and beat on that house; and it did not fall, for it was founded on the rock. But everyone who hears these sayings of Mine, and does not do them, will be like a foolish man who built his house on the sand: and the rain descended, the floods came, and the winds blew and beat on that house; and it fell. And great was its fall."

The storm is coming. You can have confidence in the face of what looks to everyone else like a great terror. But you can have that confidence only if you have built your house — that is, your life — on the unmovable Rock of Jesus Christ.

THE THING ABOUT GOD'S JUDGMENT

Daniel's life beautifully illustrates the most amazing aspect of God's judgment. Throughout eternity — yesterday, today, and forever[5] — He remains the God who

---

5. Hebrews 13:8

is love.[6] We will never understand God's judgment if we don't see it in the light of His love.

Earlier, I quoted from Jonathon Edwards' classic sermon, "Sinners in the Hands of an Angry God." I said he was a "great evangelist, pastor, and theologian." But I don't agree with everything he said.

At one point in the sermon, Edwards tells us, "God… holds you over the pit of hell, much as one holds a spider or some loathsome insect over the fire, abhors you, and is dreadfully provoked. His wrath towards you burns like fire; he looks upon you as worthy of nothing else but to be cast into the fire."

Edwards wanted to emphasize that God does not owe us any more time for turning to Him. But he made God seem a little like a kid roasting an ant with a magnifying glass.

Peter explains that God eagerly desires to give His redemption to everyone. He wrote, "The Lord is not slack concerning His promise, as some count slackness, but is longsuffering toward us, not willing that any should perish but that all should come to repentance."[7]

God does not loathe you. He loves you.

6. 1 John 1:8
7. 2 Peter 3:9

NO GREATER LOVE

John 3:16 gives us a glimpse at God's heart of love. "For God so loved the world that He gave His only begotten Son, that whoever believes in Him should not perish but have everlasting life."

1 Timothy 2:3-4 tells us that God wants salvation for all. "For this is good and acceptable in the sight of God our Savior, who desires all men to be saved and to come to the knowledge of the truth."

In Romans 5:8, we learn that, "God demonstrates His own love toward us, in that while we were still sinners, Christ died for us."

Jesus said, "Greater love has no one than this, than to lay down one's life for his friends."[8]

Jesus often likened Himself to a shepherd. In John 10:15, He said, "I lay down My life for the sheep."

Romans 2:4 says, "The goodness of God leads you to repentance."

Love starts with Him. 1 John 4:19 says, "We love Him because He first loved us."

---

8. John 15:13

1 John 4:10 says, "In this is love, not that we loved God, but that He loved us and sent His Son to be the propitiation [or, "atoning sacrifice"] for our sins."

NOW'S THE TIME

The Holy Spirit revealed a basic truth to Peter that almost anyone who believes in God would agree with. "God shows no partiality."[9]

Human beings are obsessed with wealth, ethnicity, appearance, and things that really aren't important to God. We wish we could show no partiality. And then we fail. But God never fails.

When it comes to salvation, there are two great dangers. Danger One is the attitude that says, "I'm too wicked. God knows me too well to love me."

If you're thinking that way, you're missing the point of the cross. It's not how good or bad you have been, it's what Jesus did for you. He died in your place, taking all your sins on himself. In effect, God judged Him so that He doesn't have to judge you.

Danger Two is, if anything, even more dangerous. It's the attitude that says, "I'm not so bad. I'm a good person. I don't really need to have my sins forgiven because the

---

9. Acts 10:34

few sins I have are the fault of my parents or others. It's like the book says, *I'm Okay, I'm Okay*."

Jesus spent much of His ministry talking to people with exactly that attitude. Never killed anyone? Great. But did you ever have murder in your heart? Never committed adultery? Excellent. But did you ever have adultery in your heart? He said, "Every idle word men may speak, they will give account of it in the day of judgment."[10]

You can stand before God full of your own sinfulness, or you can turn to God the Son, Jesus, and be made eternally clean.

WITHOUT WARNING

The Bible gives us many signs that tell us how things are going to go down. They appear to be near fulfillment. The Lord wants us to be ready. The Rapture is imminent. That doesn't mean it will happen in the next few minutes, but that it could. It could happen at any time and without further warning. Are you ready?

Maybe you just don't grasp the idea of an imminent Rapture, or maybe you reject it. You still need to consider another imminent event — your death. Imminent means it could happen any time. Are you ready? You may live

---

10. Matthew 12:36

to extreme old age, but you don't know. God does not promise you another second of this life.

That's why 2 Corinthians 6:2 says, "Behold, now is the accepted time; behold, now is the day of salvation."

If you want to know that when you die, you're going to heaven, ask Christ to forgive you of your sin, and repent of your sin. What does it mean to repent? It means to make a conscious decision to make a U-turn — to turn from your sin and surrender to Christ. You can do it right now.

Pray a prayer like this one.

> Dear Lord Jesus, I admit that I am a sinner, but I want to be forgiven. Right now, I repent of my sin and unbelief. I surrender to you as LORD. I will follow You all the days of my life. In Jesus' name I pray. Amen.

If you prayed it and meant it, then you can know that you are forgiven. If you made the choice to follow Jesus, then congratulations! And welcome home! You have so much ahead of you. The closer you walk with Jesus, the more amazing your life will become.

I have a couple of recommendations. Tell someone about your decision. Saying it aloud is important. Next, find or buy a Bible. They're free on the internet.

Read it. The Gospel of John is a great place to start. Next, find a church. Look for one that believes and teaches the Bible. Be careful about churches that get weird with their demands on your life. And pray. Pray that God will help you in this awesome new life.

ANOTHER KIND OF READY

If you are what the Bible often calls, "in Christ" — if you've been born again in Him — then you will go to be with the Lord in the Rapture. Maybe you made that choice a long time ago, or maybe just now. Either way, you're ready for the Lord to come for His Church.

More than that, you're ready to face death. From here on, the fear you've been thinking about since before you remember thinking about anything... will no longer be necessary. What a relief!

Jesus gave some wonderful promises that we can hang onto, but also some important warnings. One of them is that persecution will happen to those who follow Him. Some persecution will be big, and some not so big. But as we get closer to His coming, it will grow in frequency and intensity. As America begins to experience God's judgment, life will become less comfortable for followers of Christ.

Are you ready for that? Are you ready for America's coming judgment? Is your foundation in Christ strong? Are you walking close to Him? Do you study His word, pray, and share the good news of eternal life?

Know that whatever the conditions in the world, God's promises remain true. Learn about those promises. Study His word.

Are there difficulties ahead? Yes. But for those who are in Christ, there are also wonders beyond imagination.